ski sp

ski sp🐕t run

The Enchanting World of
Skijoring and Related Dog-Powered Sports

Matt Haakenstad ◆ John Thompson

Illustrated by Jack Lunde

KISATI Ventures

Ski Spot Run: The Enchanting World of Skijoring and Related Dog-Powered Sports
by Matt Haakenstad and John Thompson
Illustrated by Jack Lunde

ISBN:0-9748011-0-0

Library of Congress Control Number: 2004090034

Book design by Wendy Holdman
Editing by Mary Brandenburg
Cover design by Jack Lunde
Cover photo (front) by K. H. Raubuch
Cover photos (back) by Tom Boyd, John Sandberg, Matt Haakenstad
Photographers (interior):
Robert C. Bergstrom (pp. 2, 3, 44)
John Gaedeke (p. 74)
Lisa Haakenstad (pp. 9, 97)
Matt Haakenstad/John Thompson (pp. 26, 29, 34, 48, 93, 94, 100, 101, 103, 104, 105, 107, 110, 111, 117, 118, 128, 161, 168, 175, 176, 177, 192)
Matt Haakenstad (pp. 116, 124, 125, 132, 136, 187)
Jack Kuntz (pp. 12, 40, 42, 81, 143, 145, 146, 148, 157)
K. H. Raubuch (pp. 2, 4, 8, 10, 15, 38, 79, 138, 139, 142, 149, 151, 155, 158)
Jay Richards (p. 21)
John Sandberg (pp. 37, 95, 96, 159, 162, 163, 164, 185)
John Thompson (p. 172)

Printed by Friesens on acid free paper

Published in the United States of America
Printed in Canada

KISATI Ventures
P.O. Box 1401
Minnetonka, MN 55345

▸ *To Lisa, for your unending support and love; and to Mom, for encouraging my interest in writing.*

—M. H.

▸ *To the memory of my mother and brother, and to my family for the inspiration to write.*

—J. T.

▸ *To "Sparky" (Nancy), for your love and support.*

—J. L.

Contents

Disclaimers

Skijoring and related dog-powered sports involve hazards and can be dangerous to you and your dog. The authors have attempted to reduce associated risks by suggesting techniques and procedures relating to safety, equipment use and training. This information is provided as a general guide, without warranty, express or implied, and is not a substitute for formal training, experience and responsible behavior. The authors specifically disclaim responsibility for any liability, loss or risk arising from the use or application of the information in *Ski Spot Run*. Because skijoring and related dog-powered sports require physical exertion, consult your physician before beginning.

Ski Spot Run contains the opinions and ideas of its authors concerning dog care. This includes, but is not limited to, suggestions concerning exercise, exposure to the elements, hydration, diet, packaged dog food, specific dog food ingredients and dog food nutritional analysis. The authors have strived to provide useful information for readers in these subjects, but are not licensed professionals or formally trained in these areas. Consult your veterinarian or other qualified professional before utilizing any of the dog care information suggested in *Ski Spot Run*.

Several product names or manufacturers have been mentioned in this book, including Velcro,® a trademark of Velcro Industries B.V.; Cordura,® a trademark of E.I. du Pont de Nemours and Company; Toughtek,® a trademark of Harrison Technologies, Inc.; and 3M,® a trademark of 3M Company. The mention of products by name is not an endorsement of a specific product, and the authors do not warrant or assume any liability for the use of products mentioned in *Ski Spot Run*.

Acknowledgments

We'd like to acknowledge and thank the following people for their contributions to *Ski Spot Run:*

Mary Brandenburg for editing and providing advice on publishing.

Wendy Holdman for text design, layout, and publishing guidance.

Bruce Jenkinson for helping with the cover design.

Bill Kloubec for input on the cover design.

Susan T. Berg for text proofing.

Lisa Haakenstad for creative input, text editing, photo sessions, publishing contacts, and topic research.

Julie Thompson for creative input, photo sessions, and feeding Matt on many occasions.

Our children Stephanie, Eric, Mark, and Annie for all the photo shoots.

To the skijorers whose pictures appear in *Ski Spot Run,* for your passion for skijoring.

To skijor club volunteers for helping beginners get started in this wonderful sport.

To mushers for sharing your knowledge of dog care and training with skijorers.

To our families for tolerating many late evenings and long weekends invested in *Ski Spot Run.*

And finally, we'd like to thank our dogs for their patience during numerous photo sessions, and for illustrating that hard work should be followed by a good meal and a nap.

CHAPTER ONE

The Beauty

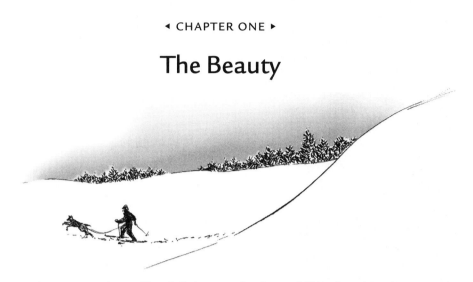

As you near the trailhead, light snow begins to fall in the crisp winter air. The sun is setting now, and the outline of trees against a purple-orange sky is breathtakingly beautiful.

Your canine companion strides gracefully in front of you as you ski, panting rhythmically as her tracks silently appear in the fresh snow. For a moment you are drawn to an earlier time when human and canine traveled together through primordial wilderness. A time when the close bond first came into being, necessitated by survival, forged with teamwork, trust and companionship. Rounding the bend for home you realize it's not so different now.

Welcome to the endearing sport of skijoring.

> *"Let us probe the silent places,*
> *Let us seek what luck betides us;*
> *Let us journey to a lonely land I know.*
> *There's a whisper on the night-wind,*
> *There's a star agleam to guide us,*
> *And the Wild is calling, calling . . . let us go."*
>
> (From *The Call of the Wild* by Robert Service)

> *"Time to get up from the PC and go off-line. I'll be on-trail."*
>
> *(Anonymous)*

Many of us seem to spend our time working, raising our kids, commuting to an office or workplace, paying bills, searching for Dilbert

K.H. RAUBUCH

ROBERT C. BERGSTROM

(and Dogbert!) in our cubicles, walking our dogs, paying taxes, waiting for spring and summer, then waiting for snow. Yes, waiting for winter.

Perhaps we won't be in the next Iditarod, or in the Nordic final at the next Olympics. But we can still get *out.* Out there, on the trail, in the weather—the snow, sleet, wind—nothing the least bit virtual about this sport. When you're skijoring, you and your dog must work together to deal with the elements. You're immersed in the experience, and that's what it's about—using your own resourcefulness and your partnership with your canine friend to challenge both the great outdoors and yourself.

Skijoring is built upon a partnership between human and animal that is unique among recreational and competitive sports. Most sports activities require either human athletic capability or athletic prowess on the part of the animal. Very few, if any, require both simultaneously, as in skijoring, where human and canine partners share the common goal of speeding down the trail and where the athletic abilities of both are important in attaining that goal.

Skijoring and mushing share several core similarities. Common themes include a profound love of dogs, the natural beauty of the outdoors, the exhilaration of a cold wind on your face, and working with and training canine athletes. A key difference between the two sports is that in mushing the human directs the activity of the dogs but does not ski along with them.

The skijoring partnership also differs from that of horseracing, where the rider or jockey is again controlling or piloting the animal. The human-equestrian bond may be incredibly strong, but the success of the team ultimately depends on the physical output of the horse. And even at a rodeo, where one may argue that the cowboy riding the bucking bronco is every bit as physically engaged as the animal, there is a difference. The bronco and cowboy clearly have different agendas and objectives, and hence very little basis for partnership. Skijoring, on the other hand, allows the skier to both direct the operation as well as to contribute physically to its success.

ROBERT C. BERGSTROM

A First Experience with Dogs on the Trail

THOR, *future skijorer*

"My first introduction to dog-powered sports was on a sled pulled by four dogs. A friend of mine had built a sled and had offered to let me take it for a spin with his dog team. I recall that I had a strong feeling, even before I started, that this was going to become a passion for me. I found myself fantasizing about owning dogs, even before starting out! I vividly remember the intensely loud barking, crying and whining coming "from deep within" the dogs as they became excited, realizing they were about to hit the trail. This was clearly a primordial voice, not learned, but an instinctive impulse. And then suddenly it became silent, as my friend released the sled and the dogs and I were underway. The tranquil sounds of the trail provided a vivid contrast to the pandemonium only a moment earlier.

As we approached the winding river trail, I swear we were flying. I was struck by the speed and strength of my friend's dogs as they pulled me along, but I had no idea what they would do at the turn-around point. Would they reverse direction and take us back to the starting point, or would they continue on indefinitely, waiting for a command that would never come? My apprehension grew as we

neared the turnaround, since I didn't know any commands and was very much at the mercy of the dogs. I needn't have worried, as they began a well-executed turn at precisely the right spot with no assistance from me.

Somehow I sensed that this sport had instant appeal—the triad of dogs, cold weather and the beauty of the outdoors had me captivated almost immediately. My experience participating in sports gave me the confidence that I could pick up this new sport quickly (even though I had limited experience with dogs). And my love for movies and books on the Arctic, Alaska, dog sledding and Jack London's stories convinced me that this was worthy of pursuit. However I also realized that I couldn't acquire and maintain the four or more dogs necessary for dog mushing while living in the suburbs. On the other hand, my friend had mentioned this sport called ski-joring, which required only one or two dogs. It seemed like the perfect way to enter the world of dog-powered sports.

By the time we returned to the trailhead, I realized I was hooked and would need to begin my quest for knowledge of dogs and the sport of skijoring. Equally important was the need to begin the task of convincing my family and friends that I hadn't lost my mind and that this was in fact the logical next step. The call of the wild was beckoning."

A Kid's First Skijoring Experience
ERIC, a 6th grader

Skijoring is a fun sport which I do with my dad. Skijoring is just like dogsledding but you get pulled really fast on skis. One or more dogs can pull you on your skis, and some people even use three dogs. I wear a skijoring belt around my waist and then two straps go through my legs. The belt connects to a line called the towline which hooks up to the dogs' harnesses. Normally I use my cross-country skis for skijoring.

I remember when my dad asked, "Do you want to try skijoring for the first time?" Since I still had a lot of energy after school and I wanted to try skijoring, I said yes. My dad was pretty excited and said "You'll have lots of fun." After we got all of the supplies in the car, including our dogs Timber and Kiska, we took off to a park. On the way there, we talked about how if you have to stop fast, you just fall or pull the quick-release so the dogs will stop pulling.

When we got there, I was revved up and ready to go skijoring. We took our skis and gear to the trail. Then we took out our dogs. After we got all of our stuff on and Kiska hooked up to me, I was ready to go. All I needed was one simple command and that was LET'S GO! After I said that, I felt a jerk and a rush of speed from Kiska. As I was going, I could feel the cold wind against my face, and then there was silence. About halfway through, I fell on the soft snow, but only once. It didn't hurt—I just slid a few feet. After our run my dad came up and asked, "Did you have fun?" I said, "Yes!" Now I'm doing it more often and even racing against grown-ups.

This book is an introduction to the amazing sport of skijoring, which combines the exhilaration of cross-country skiing, the lure of mushing, and the convenience of owning a single dog. In the following chapters we will outline the basics of the sport, with a discussion of equipment, dogs, training and technique. Along the way we'll also cover skijor racing and warm weather alternatives like canicross, bikejoring and rollerjoring, as well as volunteer and promotional opportunities. And since skijoring often includes a bit of comic relief, we've added a healthy dose of humor from both the human and canine perspectives. Was Murphy's Law originally written with skijoring in mind? Read on to form your own hypothesis!

SIBERIAN
HUSKY

CHAPTER TWO

The Sport

What is Skijoring?

ski·jor·ing (skē jôr ing,) *n.* [modif. of Norw *skikjøring,* from ski + *kjøring,* driving]: a winter sport in which a person wearing skis is drawn over snow by a dog or horse. The most common pronunciation is probably "SKIjoring," though "skiJORing, SKIjuring, and skiJURing" are also encountered. Occasionally one also hears "skiYORing." The Norwegians say "sheSHURing." Our advice: don't let uncertainty over pronunciation keep you from discussing or attempting this sport!

Winter Excitement

Skijoring is an invigorating and fast growing winter sport that combines cross-country skiing and dog mushing. Originating in Scandinavia and literally meaning "ski-driving" in Norwegian, skijoring allows a dog and owner to exercise together while enjoying the outdoors. Imagine yourself on a beautiful winter's day gliding behind your canine best friend on a tree-lined trail.

Poodles to Pointers

Virtually any breed dog can learn to skijor. Northern breeds like Alaskan huskies, malamutes and Siberian huskies have traditionally been used for skijoring due to their instinctive desire to pull, but any dog that loves to run is a good skijoring candidate. For example, the German shorthaired pointer and variations of the breed are very popular in Europe. In fact, for recreational skijoring, dog characteristics and personality are just as important as breed. If your dog is energetic and weighs 30 pounds or more, she or he may make a great skijoring dog. This is especially true if your dog enjoys pulling in front on walks or runs.

Minimal Equipment

Part of skijoring's beauty lies in its simplicity and minimal equipment requirements. Besides basic cross-country ski gear, only three

items are necessary to skijor: a harness for your dog; a skijoring belt for your waist; and a towline to connect you to your dog. For

Dog Harness

skijorers in warmer climates (or for off-season use), this equipment also functions well for canicross, bikejoring, rollerjoring (inline skating) or scootering with your dog.

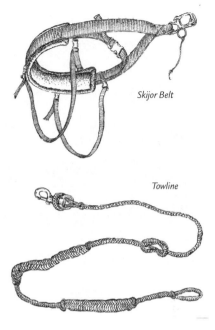

Skijor Belt

Canine Ecstasy

Dogs love to skijor. They enjoy the exercise, meeting other dogs, outdoor scents, occasional wildlife encountered and of course, companionship with their owners. From a dog's perspective, skijoring is as much fun as a walk times ten. If your dog jumps up and down when the leash comes out, just wait until she discovers what the harness foretells! Your dog will probably develop a strong Pavlovian (conditioned) response to your skijor equipment, so avoid handling the harness or towline until you're ready to use it.

Towline

From Recreation to World Championships

Skijoring has something for everyone and can be broken down into five general categories: *recreational skijoring, skijor sprint racing, skijor distance racing, backwoods skijoring* and *pulka*. Technically speaking, pulka is not a category of skijoring; rather, pulka and skijoring combined are referred to as Nordic-style mushing. Each category provides unique challenges and rewards for its participants, but one theme resonates throughout—skijorers love their dogs and enjoy spending time with them outdoors.

Recreational skijorers make up the largest segment of the sport. They typically own one dog—the family pet—and try to get out skijoring once every week or two. If there's a skijor club in their area, they might attend a pre-

Ready for canicross

LISA HAAKENSTAD

season seminar and participate in a few fun runs during the winter season. With recreational skijoring, the emphasis is on fun, fitness and camaraderie between dog and owner. Interestingly enough, many recreational skijorers learn to ski so they can skijor with their dog!

Do you enjoy the wilder rides at Six Flags, Disneyworld, or your local amusement park? If so, *skijor sprint racing* is for you. Reaching speeds close to 30 mph out of the starting chute, top sprint skijorers can average over 20 mph during a five-mile race. They race on ultralight skate skis in skin suits and have up to three race-bred dogs harnessed to them at once. Just watching the frenzied, adrenaline charged dogs at the start is exciting; imagine what it's like being tied to them! Sprint skijorers' dogs are specially bred, impeccably cared for and carefully trained.

Skijor distance racing combines the romanticism of racing sled dogs in the wilderness with the benefits of endurance conditioning for skijorer and dog team. Typically racing distances of 20 miles or more, skijor distance racers must carry survival gear and have a

thorough understanding of their dogs' nutritional needs and reaction to the elements. A working knowledge of winter survival is necessary before participating in a distance event. Dogs with shorter coats may require additional clothing or equipment to stay warm and avoid frostbite.

If you enjoy winter camping, you'll find *backwoods* or *backcountry skijoring* with your dog even more rewarding. Backcountry skijorers are drawn to the beauty and solitude of nature and often skijor on ungroomed trails far from urban development. Equipment for this type of skijoring is unique, with wider, classical-style backcountry skis and poles being the norm. If overnight excursions are planned, the use of a small sled, or pulk, is recommended for carrying gear. Any breed of dog has the potential to perform well in the backcountry, but larger breeds such as the Malamute are often preferred for their size, strength, and coat. Like distance skijoring, a thorough knowledge of winter survival is necessary before heading into the backcountry. Knowing how your dog is affected by long-term exposure to the outdoors is critical.

Pulka driving is skijoring with a small sled (pulk) attached between skijorer and dog. The pulk is preferred over a backpack for carrying heavier loads over a distance, and for this reason pulks are common among backcountry skijorers and distance racers. In Scandinavia pulka driving is very popular among racers and the general public. Children are often given rides in pulks specifically designed to carry them. Pulks can be pulled by a skijorer instead of

Pulka   Not Pulka

a dog by attaching longer shafts that connect to a modified skijoring belt. Pulka driving and skijoring share a world championship organized by the International Federation of Sled-Dog Sports. Skijoring owes its beginnings to the sport of pulka.

Skijoring Background and History

Skijoring may seem like a new arrival on the winter sports scene, but it has actually been around for over a century. How did this marriage of dogs and their people come about?

Dogs have been barking in the Arctic for years, developing a long and close association with humans in that part of the world. One estimate suggests that dogs have been used in the Far North for hauling sleds and gear for at least 12,000 years. The bond itself between canine and human may even reach back as far as 30,000 years. In recent times, author Jack London's *Call of the Wild,* and tales like the legend of Balto have through the years captured and portrayed the common theme of sled dog as friend and faithful companion.

And humans have been strapping skis on their feet for thousands of years in Norway and Sweden. The word "ski" comes from the Norwegian word "skith," which means either "snowshoe" or "strip of wood." Wooden skis found in Sweden have been dated to 3000 B.C., and skiing motifs have been found on ancestral Norwegian drums that were played about 5000 B.C. Early Scandinavians used skiing primarily as a means of transport while hunting, since it gave them an advantage in pursuing their prey. While early Nordic enthusiasts' equipment hardly resembled that available today—the skis appear to be twice the size of the traveler—the basic principles involved have remained much the same.

So it was not really a quantum leap when someone decided to combine canine pulling power with human mobility on skis. This probably happened about a century ago, though early skijoring was also done with horses. The equestrian version of skijoring persists today with a limited following, since it requires special training and safety precautions. Skijoring has also been performed behind cars and snowmobiles, but these motorized variations will not be addressed in this text. Skijoring is most popular (and probably safest!) when done behind dogs.

Skijoring's 100-year history seems brief, compared to more established winter sports such as alpine (downhill) and Nordic (cross-country) skiing. Many persons learning to skijor are dog owners from one or both of these categories of skiing. Still others either own a dog but have never skied or have skied but don't have a dog.

On the other hand, most of the dogs learning to skijor are less concerned with the alpine or Nordic comparison. They simply have an innate interest in the trail, or just enjoy the fresh air, exercise and extra rations.

Outside of Alaska and many of the Canadian provinces, skijoring is most popular in the northern one-third of the U.S., as well as areas having mountainous terrain. The warm-weather alternatives to skijoring (such as bikejoring or canicross, discussed in Chapter 9) can be enjoyed anywhere that trail access is available—creating opportunities in all 50 states and around the world.

Skijoring options vary greatly by community, depending on the availability of trails, their suitability for running with dogs, and the receptiveness and tolerance of the community toward sharing trails with dogs. Please be a good "skijoring ambassador" and check with the appropriate management authority before running your dog on ANY trail. In general, the best trails are usually found at:

- City, county or state parks
- Rails-to-trails projects
- Forest service roads
- Golf courses
- Private trail networks (resorts, clubs, etc.)
- Multi-use trails (biking, snowmobile, horse, etc.)
- Frozen lakes (make sure they are safe!)

Skijoring is emerging as an ingenious solution to that widely experienced northern phenomenon known as "cabin fever." The long, cold nights of midwinter can take their toll on even the most stalwart snow lovers. Humans and their pets have devised similar strategies for confronting this issue, sometimes involving comfortable furniture. Unfortunately, regular use of a couch to hole-up, pork out or curl up can produce an undesirable result—out-of-shape hu-

BEFORE... AFTER...

man and canine companions. Enter skijoring, and suddenly both have a common mission—to get outside and get moving!

It's probably no surprise that the exercise and fresh air afforded by skijoring benefit dog and skier alike. What may be less obvious to newcomers to the sport is the enthusiasm that most dogs have for the activity. In many cases, a dog that has skijored several times will become greatly excited by the sight of the skijoring harness and towline, sometimes to the extent that care must be taken to display the gear only when an outing is sure to follow. Those who subscribe to the myth that dogs in skijoring harness are being "worked" for the sole benefit of their owners should consider these points: 1) Effective skijoring requires nearly equal effort from both dog and skier and 2) The vast majority of dogs truly enjoy being able to run and pull and don't see it as "work" at all.

The Human—Canine Partnership

Skijoring is made possible by a partnership between human and dog. As in many relationships, both parties have certain expectations of and responsibilities toward each other. It is not always an equal partnership, since your dog must always know that you are the leader and are in control. You also have the ultimate responsibility for looking out for the best interests of yourself, your dog and other trail users. But as long as you deliver on your portion of the agreement, your dog will develop even greater respect and admiration for you. This will allow both partners to pursue their common love of the physical activity in the great outdoors, and the partnership will thrive.

Another link between dogs and people is their need to be in motion. Both species are really built for movement and are optimized through exercise. Most of us are familiar with the benefits of "going for a walk"—even a brief excursion can clear one's head and reduce stress. Norwegian sociologist and sports philosopher Gunnar Breivik suggests that many of us think more clearly when we are in motion, or at least are more prone to flashes of inspiration when we move. His view is that motion is a more natural state for man than rest, and he cites the Greek peripatetic (traveling on foot) school and Nietzsche's seminal hikes in the Alps in support of this position.

Is it any wonder that stress and ergonomic concerns abound in the workplace, with its sedentary and cubicle-oriented setting? We've yet to hear about any carpal tunnel problems that have developed on the skijoring trail. Similarly, the only downsizing we've observed so far has been of two varieties: 1) The natural loss of a pound or two that may happen for skijorer and dog as a result of their habit and 2) The temporary loss of clothing or other personal effects that sometimes occurs as one "heats up" on the trail.

But, you say, my dog seems to love to lie on the couch. And our vernacular is full of expressions like "you lazy dog." How do we reconcile this perception? Very simply—dogs have survived and flourished by being very adaptable creatures. It may help to envision them as a sort of clay that you are able to mold (this may sound familiar to parents). If you give your dog options that are mostly sedentary, she will make the most of it and attempt to serve you well. Conversely, if your dog understands that, at least periodically, she is expected to walk, run or skijor, she will embrace this as a normal part of her routine and may even harass you if you begin to slack off on her regular dose of activity. Sometimes this last point— that of having someone to remind you to get up off the couch— makes all the difference.

Skijoring is a lot like life itself in that it's a journey, not a destination. Yes, it helps immensely to set goals and objectives to guide one toward a desired end result or level of proficiency. But the real fun is in getting there, since destinations can be elusive and capricious. And put another way, some days the skis and/or the dogs just don't cooperate.

In the spirit of the human-canine partnership, the stories and testimonials scattered throughout this book attempt to address both the human and canine point of view. They are also dedicated to those days when things don't go exactly as planned, or indeed when they don't even come close. Days such as these demonstrate the importance of a healthy sense of humor. In fact, for many skijorers, being able to laugh about the inevitable mishaps of the sport may be as important as technique. We've highlighted a few of the common predicaments encountered by skijorers and their dogs, in the hope that you'll recognize them in time to avoid them. On the other hand, if you find yourself caught up in one of these scenarios, perhaps you might enjoy a good chuckle over it.

Over the course of several seasons mock interviews were conducted with five fictitious characters willing to share their chronicles. Though fabricated, these perspectives are based on observed comments and behavior. The authors wish to express their gratitude to Thor and Helga (our human interviewees), to Spot, Ginger and Bowser (our canine interviewees), and to their own dogs for serving as translators in the canine interviews.

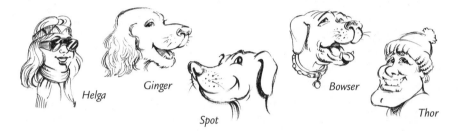

Helga   Ginger   Bowser   Thor

Spot

The canine and human motivation for hitting the trail may be different, as well as the olfactory experience (imagine cruising the

On the Trail
HELGA

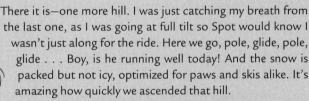

There it is—one more hill. I was just catching my breath from the last one, as I was going at full tilt so Spot would know I wasn't just along for the ride. Here we go, pole, glide, pole, glide . . . Boy, is he running well today! And the snow is packed but not icy, optimized for paws and skis alike. It's amazing how quickly we ascended that hill.

Up over the crest, and now down the other side—a squirrel—ON BY! Good dog." Now we're flying, Spot running like the wind, and me controlling my descent behind. We're at the bottom in record time, invigorated by the fresh cold air. We both lean into the curves on the flats. He's running wide open now, and I'm skating and poling behind. We're in sync and melodious as we head into the straightaway. Then it's into the parking area—I do believe he knows where the water and more treats are stashed.

trail with a sense of smell amplified several hundred times!). But it's not by chance that the bond between dogs and their owners has persisted for perhaps 30 millennia. In addition to this important bond, the sport of skijoring offers the potential for other partnerships beyond the teaming of dog and human.

Partnering is also fostered by the need for trails and has resulted in sometimes delicate alliances between skijorers and interest groups such as snowmobilers, cross-country skiers, bicyclists, equestrians, hikers and rails-to-trails advocacy groups. Cross-seasonal relationships tend to be more complementary and are perhaps somewhat easier to sustain. For example, skijorers and mountain bikers can fairly easily share the same stretch of trail, since their trail use occurs during different seasons (yet both groups can band together to maintain trails and address encroaching development). Skijorers and cross-country skiers, however, have a more challenging situation, since their trail use occurs during the same season. Chapter 7 (Stewardship) provides suggestions for working with other groups as allies to increase trail access and quality for all concerned.

And finally, a lighter-side vignette, observed recently, reminds us of the wide range of people and personalities that can be experienced when skijoring.

The Skijoring Clampetts Roll into Town

The scene: a parking lot packed with skijorers' minivans, dog trucks (pickups fitted with dog boxes), sedans and sport utility vehicles, adjacent to the starting point for a series of skijoring and mushing races. Skijorers and dogs alike are busy with their prerace rituals of laying out harnesses, lines, skis and poles; chatting about trail conditions, start order, and the correct "wax du jour;" setting watches to official race time; last-minute "dropping" of dogs; and listening to the announcer rattling off an unending stream of information.

At first, the rumbling sound is off in the distance, just barely audible. A cloud of dust traces its way along the gravel road leading into the parking lot, a miniature dark cloud wafting across the prairie. Dog and human alike are momentarily distracted by the growing form on the southern horizon. Someone murmurs "What is THAT?" as curious dogs and owners occasionally glance at the emerging source of the disturbance.

Eventually a dilapidated old Chevy Suburban lumbers into view, coughing and sputtering as it bounces into the parking lot. The antithesis of a new car advertisement, the decaying hulk exudes a mix of earth-tone colors, chief among them a rusty brown. Someone has scrawled "WASH ME" in the dust above the Wall Drug and Reptile Gardens stickers plastered across the rear bumper. Patches of faded duct tape can be discerned in strategic locations, doing their best to hold onto a door panel here, a taillight there. The roof of the vehicle is piled high with industrial-size bags of dog food, mushing gear, dog kennels and an old mattress. The occupants, never seen before or since, are later dubbed "the Clampetts" by those in attendance. They have earned a place in local mushing and skijoring lore.

Inside the vehicle there is a beehive of activity. The entire family has apparently come along for this event—Ma, Pa and a brood of three or four young 'uns. The inside of the vehicle is also crammed with the accoutrements of dog mushing. Indeed, several of these artifacts are visible—a dog sled protruding from an open window, a harness flapping from a closed door and dragging on the road, a

snow hook pinched between the tailgate and the closed rear window. But the real treat is the six dogs swarming around inside the vessel, in constant motion between bow and stern, barking, howling and scratching to get out. The human occupants seem oblivious to this canine cacophony as they sit impassively. A cloud of dust and debris accompanies the vehicle—perhaps Charles Shultz would have described the contraption as "Pigpen on Wheels."

The Suburban fishtails to a stop in a corner of the parking lot, and the doors are immediately forced open by the discharging occupants and cargo. Burger wrappers, dog booties, French fry containers, ski poles and crumpled Coke cans tumble out the open doors. The Clampetts and their canine entourage emerge, catching all of those present with eyes wide and mouths open. The driver (some call him "Jed") breathes a loud sigh of relief and exclaims "By gum, Granny, I think we got us a dawg race." Everyone returns to prerace preparations, slightly embarrassed at being caught staring, but each resolving to be present at the starting line when the Clampett's turn arrives.

CHAPTER THREE

The Technique

Skijoring is a safe sport for skijorer and dog when practiced responsibly. Because skijoring involves both speed and the outdoors, there are some variables that cannot be completely controlled. Thus, it is important to understand the associated risks before beginning. A number of basic safety tips are included here to help you understand and manage the various risks (and to have more fun!).

Ski lesson in progress

Learn to Ski before Skijoring

Basic skiing skills are necessary to begin skijoring. You should be able to maintain your balance, snowplow proficiently, and feel comfortable climbing and descending hills. Snowplowing is important for holding your dog in place while making last-minute adjustments to equipment before starting, and slowing your dog as necessary on the trail. More proficient skijorers sometimes incorporate a hockey stop (a sideways stop) into their routine.

Experienced skijorers will also step corners and carve turns. Both methods are used to execute a turn while maintaining an efficient line through the corner. Stepping maintains or even increases speed, while carving reduces speed. Note that it is unnecessary to employ all of these techniques to begin skijoring.

Many people have heard about or observed skijoring and want to try the sport. In some cases they'll purchase skijoring equipment such as the harness, belt and towline along with skiing gear, without ever having attempted skiing. We would suggest a more gradual immersion, such as renting or borrowing skis, or perhaps taking a basic lesson, so that you can first experience the beauty of cross-country skiing. Your chances of success are enhanced if you are able to ski at a basic level prior to adding dog plus skijor gear. If you like skiing, you're bound to love skijoring, but we do learn to walk before we learn to run.

Work on some of the fundamentals of skiing before moving on to skijoring. Practice moving down the trail and around turns and obstacles while maintaining your balance. Make sure you can slow down and stop, using a snowplow stance or other techniques. Try to get a sense for what it's like to ski in varying conditions—new snow, icy trail, crusty or granular snow, etc. How are your speed and control affected? As you round turns and climb and descend hills, envision what adjustments you might make if you had a dog pulling up front. Remember that adding a dog will increase speed, especially on corners and downhill sections.

The two broad categories of cross-country (or Nordic) skiing are classic/diagonal stride skiing, and skate/freestyle skiing. Classic skiing has been around for many years, and utilizes a walking motion along a track for each ski. Though no longer as popular among racers, classic skiing is still the most popular form of the sport for the general public.

Skate skiing (or simply skating) became popular following Olympian Bill Koch's innovative use of the technique. It requires a type of trail different from that for classic cross-country skiing. Skate skiing is done on a groomed or compacted surface without tracks for the individual skis. Many trails are groomed for both classic skiing and skate skiing. A skate skier actually skates along the trail, using a motion much the same as one would use when ice skating. Classic and skating skis, boots and poles are slightly different in form and function. Hybrid models attempt to satisfy the requirements of both skiing methods. Visit a local ski shop to learn more about ski equipment.

Skijoring is actually done using either form of cross-country skiing, depending on skier preference, trail conditions and desired speed. Both methods are widely used, and local trail availability is the deciding factor for many skijorers. The following summary may be useful in comparing the two techniques:

Classic/Diagonal

- A versatile method—works on any type of trail, including classic, skate, narrow, or no trail at all

- Most popular ski method for beginner and recreational skijorers, also used by experienced skijorers when backcountry skijoring or in areas that lack skate trails

- Essentially walking on skis, making this an easy technique to learn

- Waxless classic skis are available that require minimal maintenance

- Equipment is widely available in most geographic areas

- *Note:* skijorers should not allow their dogs to run in the machine-groomed tracks

Skate/Freestyle

- Offers greater speed than classic

- Provides improved maneuverability and control at higher speeds

Classic trail

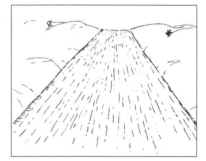
Skate trail

Combined trail

- Requires a trail groomed specifically for skating, or snow depths of less than three inches; a skate trail is wider than classic—seven-or eight-foot minimum width

- Skate skis require regular waxing for optimal performance

Skating dominates the racing scene because of its speed and inherent efficiency. The walking/striding motion of classic skiing is replaced with a lateral motion, and the gliding action of skating can significantly increase traveling speed.

Spread Eagle Stop

THOR

This maneuver is also known as the "face-plant" or "head-plant" and seems to occur when the skijorer is moving at full throttle down the trail, and the dog (for whatever reason) moves abruptly at a right angle to the trail. The skijorer's attempts to stop or change direction lead to crossed ski tips, resulting in a chest-first landing on the snow. This tactic can sometimes provide a "free flight" experience—in the instant before hitting the snow, I'm an astronaut, training in a steep-descent airplane. . . .

It's definitely an effective stop, since movement does tend to cease once the skier is sprawled out on the snow. It can also be quite entertaining for observers. This trick usually brings a quizzical look from your dog.

Safety Tips and Procedures

Know what to do when your dog suddenly lunges against a slack towline.
On occasion the towline may go slack, and then snap tight as your dog accelerates. This may happen if you stop to undo a tangle, or when you're starting down the trail. You should anticipate and prepare for the resulting jerk when the line tightens, especially if you have a dog with lots of pulling power. Please, do NOT stand up straight and lean back or attempt to resist the tension. This caveat is even more critical when skijoring with more than one dog.

Instead, simply bend forward at the waist and assume a downhill ski tuck position so that your back is nearly parallel to the ground. This stance may seem strange or even awkward at first, but once you've tried it, you will immediately incorporate it into your arsenal of tricks. The secret here is that this position transfers nearly all of your dog's pulling force and jerking motion directly to your hips, posterior and legs, instead of to your lower back. Put another way, this position aligns your spine with the force vectors generated by your dog's motion, compared to being at a 90-degree angle if you were to stand up straight. Once the shock force has been absorbed, you may stand up and resume normal skijoring motion. This simple maneuver is nearly 100% effective at reducing the risk of serious back problems from sudden towline shock.

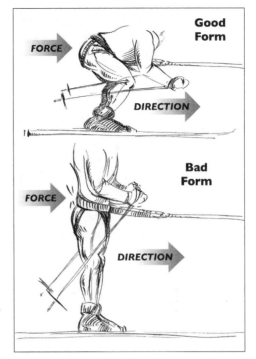

Assume a ski tuck position if your dog lunges against a slack towline.

Understand how your skijoring equipment works. In particular, practice releasing and reconnecting your quick-release snap several times before hooking up your dog. The quick-release should remain attached to the skijor belt upon release. This will prevent the quick-release from chasing your dog down the trail or swinging wildly on the end of the towline.

Wear a helmet if conditions warrant: for example, when skijoring on a trail with downhill turns and trees. If unsure about whether conditions justify a helmet, just wear the helmet. A bike helmet works well. Otherwise you could wear a downhill-ski helmet or hockey helmet. Wear impact-resistant eyewear (sunglasses or goggles) to avoid eye injury from branches, brush, etc., as well as snow and ice kicked up by your dog. Protective eyewear becomes even more essential if you have fast-running dogs.

Avoid trails with motorized vehicle traffic, such as snowmobiles, whenever possible. If you must use the same trail, choose a time

Reflective gear

when traffic is light and wear bright clothing. During low light conditions, use reflective gear for you and your dog. Add a head-lamp for increased visibility. Identify blind spots on the trail where motor vehicle operators may not see you.

Do not skijor on lakes, ponds or rivers until you are absolutely certain the ice is safe. If you are unsure, contact the Department of Natural Resources or a similar agency in your area.

Always tell at least one person where you're going and when you expect to return. This is especially important for backcountry skijoring. Do not attempt backcountry skijoring or winter camping unless you are well versed in winter survival and have all the necessary gear.

There is safety in numbers. Skijoring by yourself may be okay on your local golf course, but don't travel alone in remote or wilderness areas.

Children should not skijor without adult supervision. Even your normally docile family pet may become very excited on the trail and pull with surprising force. Kids can do quite well at skijoring once they've mastered the basics, but they should always be closely supervised. A conservative and safe trail for their first outing helps leave a positive first impression.

Never wrap a towline or neckline around your fingers, wrist, leg, neck, or any other part of your body. An excited dog can pull with substantial force and could cause injury.

THOR

I was skijoring with both Spot and Bowser several years ago, when they were still pups. It was a brisk, clear day, and the dogs were full of adrenaline. They knew the meandering trail through the woods and needed no encouragement from me to rocket along. I looked forward to the scenic section past the old wooden bridge that crossed an icy, thundering stream.

The bridge was now coming up quickly—time to decelerate. I noticed that we had moved out of the sheltered, forested area and were now on windswept tundra. I attempted to set an edge on my right ski in a snowplow vee, but it refused to grip the icy surface at all—a stark contrast to the forgiving snow at the trailhead. I tried a full snowplow with both skis, with no luck. It seemed that any attempt at braking caused me to lose control. I'd guess we were running close to 25 mph.

I was now pretty alarmed and figured that my best shot lay in staying calm and maintaining control as we crossed the bridge. My goal was simple: avoid

continued on next page

THE TECHNIQUE ◄ 27

continued from previous page

crashing into the railing or shooting over the edge into the stream below. Out I blasted onto the bridge, striving to stay centered by focusing on my dogs and ignoring peripheral glances toward the frigid waters. Like a runaway semi-trailer barreling down a mountain canyon, we weaved and rocked over the uneven bridge, but successfully traversed the crossing.

My elation was short-lived, however, as I knew what lay ahead. The sharp 90-degree turn loomed, and I again attempted to slow down. WHOA! WHOA! I cried, but my dogs were still learning and besides, they were cookin'!! I tried dragging my poles, without success. I again tried my best snowplow, but the icy surface was frictionless. In desperation, I stood high and tried to flare out my body and jacket into a sort of parachute, but this had minimal effect since we were going with the wind. Now very concerned about the dogs' and my own personal safety, I scanned the edges of the trail for any soft snow that would suit a crash landing. We were out on the windswept tundra, so there was none.

As we entered the turn, I tried snowplowing and surprisingly, made it around the turn. For an instant my mind drifted back, recalling this sensation from a summer day on an inner tube behind a speedboat. The centrifugal force intensified as I came out of the turn, producing a slingshot effect. This time I went flying, head over heals, with skis and poles scattering in several directions. A piece of my ski binding whizzed past my ear. I came down hard on my elbow, grimacing as I swiftly contemplated whether or not it was broken. I saw one ski hurtling above the icy surface, as if in slow motion, exuberant in its newfound yet fleeting freedom.

It seemed like a long time before I sat up and surveyed the damage. My dogs had returned to my side, curious about why I had decided to stop. No, the elbow didn't seem broken but would surely be sore for a few days. I gathered up my gear and began the long trek back to the car on foot. I didn't want to risk further injury to myself or the dogs. Spot and Bowser dashed ahead off-leash, somewhat perplexed by the change of plans but good sports nonetheless.

I learned several important lessons that day:

1. Never ski in conditions where there may be danger to you or your dogs.

2. When making this judgment, consider the entire trail, not just the initial segment. This particular trail had started out innocently enough as a forested, protected path with adequate snowpack and texture.

3. If unsure about either of the first two points, ski the route first by yourself. It's far easier to control your own flight path when you don't have to worry about your dogs in front of you.

Start out skijoring with a single dog. Do not skijor with more dogs than you can control. Even if you have two dogs, begin with one on a flat, straight trail without obstacles. Beginners should have someone present to help.

If unsure about the trail, ***ski the trail first without your dog*** to assess the trail condition, difficulty and potential for danger (for example, a steep downhill or road crossing). If you have any control problems whatsoever on this solo run, keep in mind that they will only be magnified with your dog.

Remember to "water" your dog. One of the challenges facing any athlete is making sure that fluid consumption is adequate. Dogs are no different, and like humans, they can enter the early stages of dehydration before becoming thirsty. More to the point, they depend on you as the source of hydration (unless you happen to be passing an open lake or stream). You'll probably recall from your own experience that it is

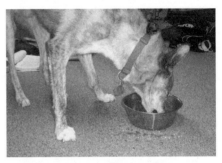

Don't forget cool water after the run

much easier to think ahead and ward off dehydration by drinking enough water than it is to deal with the effects of dehydration. Always give your dog plenty of opportunities to drink—before, during and after your run. Your dog's fluid intake will depend on your dog's size and individual characteristics. Water should be cool in temperature, but not cold.

If your dog won't drink, or drinks very little, try baiting the water with something your dog will relish. This is an effective trick used by racers to entice their dogs to imbibe. For example, adding a small amount of tuna juice and tuna, or cooked hamburger bits, etc., to your dog's water bowl will make it irresistible (to your dog, though perhaps not to you). This procedure will encourage her to drink when she otherwise might not. Glucose replenishment drinks similar to those used by human athletes are also available for dogs. These products can increase performance and reduce recovery time, but they are not a substitute for daily water intake.

Pay close attention to feeding. Provide your dog a good quality dog food that is free of artificial preservatives such as BHA/BHT or ethoxyquin, artificial colors or flavors, and byproducts (like beaks, feet or entrails). We suggest a 30% protein/20% fat mix for very active dogs and 25% protein/15% fat ratio for active recreational dogs. Ingredients are listed in order of weight, and the first one listed should be meat, poultry or fish. Don't be misled by slick marketing—compare ingredients and the American Association of Feed Control Officials (AAFCO) percentages on the side of the bag. Store your dog food in a cool, dry area.

Start with the feeding guidelines suggested on the bag and adjust for your dog's activity level, age, target weight and weather conditions. You may want to supplement your dog food with meat or fish if your dog has been in a hard-working mode. If your dog eats fast and coughs up food, try feeding in several smaller portions that have been moistened with water. If switching to a new dog food, do so gradually over a one-week period. Record your dog's weight before the switch. Your vet will be able to advise you on the proper weight for your dog.

Dog Jacket

Be prepared for changing weather conditions. Take an extra outer shell jacket for yourself and a dog jacket for your dog if she has a light coat or fine fur (dogs experience windchill, too!). Always expect the weather to change for the worse on extended outings. And to avoid overheating in warmer weather, keep your runs short when the temperature is above 40 degrees Fahrenheit.

Introduce your dog to skijoring gradually, so your dog has fun gaining fitness and looks forward to the next trip. By limiting your initial skijoring sessions to 10 or 15 minutes, you'll keep the skijoring experience positive for your dog. Because skijoring is also a workout for the skijorer, a measured introduction makes sense for the skier as well. And, your skijoring experiences will be more enjoyable if you build a good fitness base.

Do not skijor with metal-edged skis, since they can injure your dog if contact is made from behind. Metal edges add weight and are of little use on a groomed ski trail, so don't risk severing an artery in your dog's leg.

Know the trail surface. If you're skijoring on a trail that has pavement underneath, make sure there's adequate snowpack to protect your dog's feet from excessive pad and toenail wear. Feel the snow on the trail with your bare hands to test the consistency. If the snow has thawed and frozen several times without being groomed, the trail may feel sharp and crunchy. In this case you should put booties on your dog to prevent abrasions. Don't risk loss of control or injury to you or your dog by skijoring on an icy trail.

If you see any red snow behind your dog, stop immediately and check your dog's feet for abrasions. Always carry a set of booties for each dog.

Booties

Don't skijor when your dog is sick. Take special care when your dog shows symptoms of illness. There is a double incentive not to run when your dog is not feeling well. First, your dog will probably not have a good time, may not perform well and may risk injury or more serious illness if forced to push herself. Second, in a racing environment or public setting, you could spread a virus to other dogs.

Never leave your dog unattended while harnessed or leashed, especially at a race. And don't let your dog run off leash around other dogs or people in a race setting. Keep your dog separated from other dogs unless contact is mutually agreed upon.

Don't run into your dog from behind. If snowplowing doesn't slow your speed sufficiently to avoid hitting your dog from behind, steer to either side, use the hockey stop or fall down. You should avoid hitting your dog from behind at all costs.

Be aware of the potential for frostbite which can occur on ears, genitals or teats. Signs of recent frostbite can include a scaly appearance to the dog's skin, along with a preoccupation with or licking of the affected area by the dog. In advanced stages, the skin may turn black and fall off. Any part of the dog not covered with fur is vulnerable. Breeds with short hair or light coats are particularly susceptible, so pay special attention to changing conditions that could put your dog at risk. Recent surgery can also increase frostbite potential, if the area was shaved prior to the procedure.

When you stop moving, attempt to find a sheltered spot, out of the wind. In normal conditions, dogs are generally fine when they're in motion due to increased body heat. It's when you stop

THOR

Bowser and I are barreling along, having just reached a full head of steam, when suddenly, there she is—a gorgeous woman, her husky on leash, standing by a tree. The two of them are just off to the left of the trail, watching us go by. The success I have controlling my urge to become acquainted is trumped when Bowser darts for the husky. Bowser, of course, goes to the left of the tree, while my momentum carries me to the right. As the towline wraps around the arboreal obstacle, it tightens, pulling Bowser against the tree and throwing me to the ground. I believe the lady already knows, as she hovers over me and intones "Are you okay?" that only my pride has suffered any wounds. "Yeah, thanks for asking. Guess I was a little slow with my ON BY command," is my timid response.

that you need to be especially careful. However, windchills below zero degrees Fahrenheit can be dangerous, whether your dog is moving or not. It pays to be extra cautious about frostbite, since body parts that have been frostbitten once are more prone to subsequent problems.

Practice good trail etiquette. Alert other skiers and skijorers when you are about to pass, and be a good ambassador for the sport by passing at a safe speed.

BOWSER

Thor and I are cruising along, with him finally getting his rhythm down so I'm not doing my usual 65% of the work. Suddenly, there she is—a gorgeous husky, her human on a leash, standing by a tree. I know Thor would never stop for introductions, so I figure I'd better take things into my own paws. Just as I'm getting close, though, I feel the line tighten and realize that humans can't corner like we can. I glance back just in time to see Thor round the tree on the other side and hit the snow. An instant later I'm pulled into the tree. The husky comes over and we get acquainted, and have a grand time sniffing around and checking out the tree while Thor slowly dusts himself off. Sometimes he can be a bit of an embarrassment.

Drop your dog before skijoring. "Dropping" your dog refers to allowing your dog to urinate, defecate or both. It's always a good idea to drop your dog in an area that you've chosen before heading out on the trail, to prevent having to attend to this a couple of minutes into your run. Also, when using a Nordic center or parking area, avoid high traffic areas when dropping your dog. Yellow-or brown-spotted snow around the entrance to a touring center is not the best advertising for skijoring. Ideally, you should stop your car before arriving at the venue or trailhead to water and drop your dogs. An added bonus is that this is usually more efficient, sans all the distractions at the trailhead.

Creative Packaging

HELGA

Some skijorers enjoy using creative packaging for recovering and transporting home any "used dog food" that their dog deposits on the trail. One inventive owner favors colorful plastic bags from several of the nation's upscale retailers. So beware—that chic plastic bag advertising expensive chocolates or designer perfume may indeed contain a surprise, though perhaps not quite of the nature you were expecting!

At a race, it is expected that dogs will be dropped at the race site. Do your best to quickly clean up after your dog, including spreading fresh snow over the soiled area when possible.

Be aware that your dog can run faster up hills than you can ski, and that you can ski faster down hills than your dog can run. Try to moderate these transitions by increasing your skiing speed or snowplowing as necessary. On descents, avoid distracting your dog by maintaining an adequate distance behind him (he'll probably look back at you if you're uncomfortably close). Following too close can cause your dog to lose confidence. Remember that an overarching goal is for your dog to not really notice that you are behind, at least in terms of either contacting your dog or forcing your dog to strain with your weight. Your objective should be to provide a uniform, manageable, constant load for your dog when possible.

It is worth repeating—do not hit your dog from behind, especially when descending hills. Doing so may require everything short of canine psychotherapy to convince your skijoring partner that you will not let it happen again. Think ahead and start snowplowing in advance. In an emergency, it's okay to pass your dog on either side or even to pull your dog with you in extreme cases. Just don't run into your dog. And as mentioned previously, avoid using metal-edged skis, which are more likely to injure your dog if accidental contact occurs.

Skijoring on hills is challenging due to the differences in speed between you and your dog. For example, when you are ascending the crest of a hill, your dog may already be accelerating on the other side's downward slope. The transition here is important, and you might want to drag your poles and snowplow slightly to provide some resistance and reassurance for your dog. This back pressure can also moderate your speed and help your dog maintain her balance. Say EASY to persuade your dog to throttle back slightly.

Skijor equipment is now available with variable rate suspension that greatly minimizes the jerking effect associated with hill transitions. The variable rate is accomplished through multiple-diameter bungee cords in the skijor belt and towline, which are specially designed to absorb a wider range of pulling forces. The new systems can provide up to three feet of elongation, which helps smooth the effects of hill transitions and even out non-synchronous movements and differences in speed between dog and skier.

Multi-diameter bungee cords

Unless you are an experienced skijorer training your dog for racing, avoid allowing your dog to run down hills at high speed. The chance of injury increases significantly from doing so, especially on steep descents. Instead, snowplow to provide back pressure against your dog's harness, which will in turn keep your dog's speed in check.

Suggested methods for varying workout intensity. There are several ways to moderate the intensity of your dog's workout. One is to vary the terrain by skijoring on trails with combinations of hills and flat stretches. For example, an easier workout might incorporate more flat sections, which are both predictable and less strenuous. Add hilly sections when you're ready for increased difficulty. In warmer weather, work output can be increased by choosing a wood chip or sandy trail versus hardpack dirt.

You can also vary the duration of the workout. Use good judgment by increasing your workout time gradually and in small increments. Another trick is to vary familiarity with the trail. Dogs (and people, for that matter!) generally won't run as intensely on a routine and familiar trail as on a new, unknown trail. An uncharted route is more exciting to dogs and will likely motivate them to run harder.

Teaching Your Dog to Pull

For thousands of years, dogs have enthusiastically helped humans transport themselves and their supplies while providing companionship and protection. In the Far North, Eskimos used dogs to pull their sleds during hunting expeditions, often traversing great distances over difficult terrain. In North America, Native Americans used  dogs to transport supplies via a travois, or drag sled, constructed of two poles and animal skin webbing. Perhaps your dog is a distant cousin to these hard working and dedicated canines.

Harnessing Natural Behavior

Every dog from poodle to Irish setter shares an ancestral link to the wolf and displays many of the same instinctive behavioral traits. For example, you may have noticed that your dog howls when a siren is heard or circles before lying down. These primordial behaviors have been passed on from generation to generation for eons and are still a powerful force in your dog's life. By tapping into instincts like these, training becomes easier for you and a natural behavior progression for your dog. In teaching your dog to pull, we suggest taking advantage of three canine instincts: chasing, trail running and pack running.

Chasing. In the wild, wolves depend on chasing for their very survival. They chase deer, moose, rabbits, lemmings, squirrels, mice, etc., as well as each other during play. It's not surprising the instinct is so ingrained in domesticated dogs today. Can your dog resist chasing a squirrel or rabbit?

When training your dog to pull, make sure your dog has something exciting to chase a short distance up the trail. Examples include a skijor or sled-dog team, a friend running with a dog, or a family member skiing or running. The keys here are sight and movement, and to some extent, scent and sound. Your dog must have the opportunity to see the chase object "running away" to ignite the chase instinct. If you don't know a skijorer or musher, contact a skijoring or mushing club in your area. Dog-powered sport enthusiasts enjoy helping those new to the sport.

Trail running. Wolves instinctively follow the path of least resistance to conserve energy, as do their prey. In the wild, they patrol well-defined game paths, often in single file with the alpha male leading. This is especially evident in winter, when travel outside the path can be extremely difficult due to deep snow. By beginning skijor training on a well-defined trail—for example, a ski trail with at least a foot-high berm on each side—you allow your dog to follow her instincts.

Since the first training session is most critical, take time to find the best available trail. For example, you may locate a marginal trail that is ten minutes away, or a much better trail that is twenty minutes farther. Particularly in the initial sessions, it will be well worth it to drive the additional twenty minutes to the better trail.

In winter, choose a one-way trail that is relatively flat and straight for safety and ease of learning. Although winding trails through the woods seem to excite dogs the most, they shouldn't be used until you're comfortable with skijoring and can control your dog. Select a time of day when you can be alone on the trail, usually early morning, and remember that a clearly defined trail is of paramount importance. One final note: choose a narrower trail over a wider one when possible. A 20-foot-wide ski trail, for example, may confuse your dog even if the berm on each side is adequate.

In non-snow seasons you'll have more trail choices because you can run behind your dog instead of ski. This sport is called canicross, and its comparative simplicity makes it a good introduction to trail running. Although experienced skijorers often train their dogs in the spring and fall using bicycles (called bikejoring), beginners should not attempt this option due to safety and control con-

Canicross

cerns. The same is true for using off road style in-line skates, referred to as rollerjoring. See Chapter 9 for more detail on these
warm-weather alternatives to skijoring.

As mentioned before, choose a flat and relatively straight one-
way trail, but consider the following differences:

- On foot you'll have better control and a lower speed than
  when skiing, so use a narrower, wooded trail if available:
  i.e., a path. Hiking trails through heavy woods or under-
  cover are a dog's favorite. This type of trail gives your dog
  the opportunity to run in only one direction (forward)
  and maximizes the instinctive trail running response.

- Avoid asphalt trails. An excited dog pulling in harness can
  literally run in place on a hard surface, wearing toenails
  and pads down quickly. Grass and dirt trails are best, followed by sand, wood chip and crushed gravel trails. Before
  running on any trail, check for sharp rocks and other hazards, and use dog booties whenever trail conditions are
  questionable.

- In non-snow seasons you must be vigilant for signs of
  heat stress in your dog, especially when temperatures are
  above 40 degrees Fahrenheit. Keep your training sessions

The pack running instinct is strong among dogs.

short and on shaded trails, and always have fresh water on hand. After your run, provide water to your dog in a shaded area with good air circulation. If you drive to the trail, roll your windows down partway or turn the air conditioner on to keep your dog cool during the ride home.

Pack running. Wolves are pack animals and work as a team to run down prey. During the hunt, they gain strength, speed and sensory acuity from a heightened physical and mental state. If you've ever competed in a running race, you've probably felt this phenomenon yourself and noticed how you can run faster and longer in a group versus on your own. Domesticated dogs experience this feeling as well, even if the only other member of their pack is the skijorer. You'll need another skijorer or musher to effectively tap into this method of training, which yields remarkable results. In essence, it's dogs teaching dogs in an energized group atmosphere.

▸ If you know an experienced skijorer or musher, ask if he would be willing to hook your dog up with one or two of his dogs for a short distance. Let him know your dog has never pulled in harness, but is well socialized and friendly. Don't try this if your dog is not. As an experienced dog driver, he'll keep the pace moderate during your dog's first run and give positive reinforcement when appropriate. Suggest meeting at a trail where the skijorer or musher regularly trains, and return the favor by helping him to the start line at his next race.

- If you have a skijoring club in your area, or a mushing club with a skijoring contingent, ask when the next seminar or "fun run" will be held. At these events you can expect to receive friendly, hands-on training and advice from knowledgeable skijoring enthusiasts. Most important, you'll have the opportunity to see the instincts related to pulling come to life in your dog. Don't be surprised if Rover takes off like Iron Will's lead dog as you chase 20 other skijor teams down the trail!

Keep the first few sessions short so your dog is still pulling hard at the end of the run, and give her positive reinforcement or a treat when you finish. Remember that the whole experience should be very positive for your dog. Once she associates the harness with skijoring, you'll be amazed at her reaction when you pull the harness out!

Dog training in general is most effective when variables are controlled, consistency is maintained and repetition is practiced. If your dog didn't take to pulling like you had anticipated, stay positive—especially when interacting with your dog—and read on.

Dogs Are the Best Teachers

Following are numerous approaches for teaching your dog to pull. The most effective techniques incorporate other dogs into the training session. This type of training is successfully used by mushers and arouses the chasing and pack running instincts in your dog. Because training with other dogs greatly increases the probability for success, it is wise to attend a skijor clinic or fun run in your area. Mushing clubs also have seminars, beginner's clinics, mentor programs, etc. Join a club and you'll find plenty of friendly people willing to help you get started.

JACK KUNTZ

Ideas for Training Your Dog to Pull

1. Attend a skijoring seminar or fun run as previously discussed. With dogs running down the trail ahead of your dog, she's almost certain to chase.

2. Hook your dog up with a skijorer's or musher's small team. This is how mushers train their young dogs to pull.

3. Have a couple of neighbors run ahead of you with their dogs on leashes. The objective here is to create an irresistible chase object for your dog. Use a well-defined trail to ignite the trail running instinct.

4. Ask family members or friends to run or ski ahead of you and your dog. Have them occasionally call your dog forward by name. Enthusiasm will work wonders.

5. Have a family member skijor as *you* run or ski in front of your dog. Your dog should be excited to chase you. Reward her with praise when she does.

6. Connect a leash to your dog's collar and have a family member hold the leash while running alongside your dog

as you skijor behind. When your dog begins pulling, the family member should begin slowing down, effectively moving your dog forward to a leading position. Reward your dog with praise for pulling and leading.

7. If you are accustomed to using treats in training, try placing one of your dog's favorite treats (liver, hamburger, etc.) about 50 yards up the trail. Show your dog where the treat is, then walk back to your skis with your dog and get ready. Your dog should be anxious to run towards the treat. If possible, have a family member hold the treat and call out your dog's name.

8. Connect a small log or small bag of sand to your dog's harness with five feet of rope, then take your dog for a

---

Keeping Your Human Focused on Pulling

GINGER

What a beautiful day for skijoring! Thor and I have just warmed up and are moving in unison. The snow surface is quite firm with adequate paw traction, ambient odor component favorable (both squirrel and deer present within a half mile radius), trail well-defined. Thor must have waxed correctly today, as I notice less drag on the line meaning I don't have to pull him as much as usual. I believe he's starting to catch on and follow my lead.

Then, all of a sudden, I notice that we're slowing dramatically and ambling in the HAW direction. Then I see the problem: there's a human (female variety) who's just taken a tumble, and Thor is stopping to assist her. Poor gal, she doesn't have a dog with her—wonder how she finds her way? In no time at all Thor has helped her up, and we're ready to return to the trail. But no, what is this? We're lingering and chatting. What am I supposed to do? Man, I was just hitting my stride, too. So I interject a couple quick "targeted barks," urging Thor to hit the trail. He glances rather disdainfully at me, says "quiet," and continues to chat about his equipment, of all things. Honestly, I love humans but I've never understood their clumsy and inefficient courtship process. They'd never survive in the wild with such tactics, but I guess that's why the great pooch in the sky gave them cities. Anyway, after several more carefully chosen but increasingly urgent barks, we're moving once again. Within 100 paces we're back in prime form. Next time I will endeavor to steer him away from such temptations, well in advance.

---

walk (with a leash attached to her collar) down a smooth path. Give your dog positive reinforcement for pulling. If your dog is reacting well, increase your pace and gradually drift behind to place your dog in a leadership position. If your dog stays up front, say, "Good Dog!" and let her continue as you remain behind.

If Your Dog Won't Pull

Don't throw in the towel just yet! The probability is still high that your dog can learn to pull. We've already discussed dogs' instinctive tendency toward pulling. Also consider that most dogs enjoy exercising outdoors with their owners, and skijoring gives them a prime opportunity for this. So don't give up hope—your dog may simply not understand that pulling is appropriate, encouraged and most important, fun.

Trained Not to Pull?

Think about pulling from your dog's perspective. Since puppy-hood your dog has been trained to heel at your side without

pulling against her collar. Now at the drop of a hat, you've changed your mind about heeling and want her to pull in front of you with reckless abandon! For a well trained dog, this can be very confusing. It may take a few outings before your dog understands that pulling in the harness is acceptable.

To help your dog differentiate between the harness and collar, use the harness exclusively for pulling-related activities, i.e., skijoring, canicross, bikejoring, etc., and never for walks, unless you expect your dog to pull. If you run with your dog, feel free to use the skijoring belt, towline and harness, but make sure your dog pulls out front (as opposed to running alongside). In sum, your dog should associate the harness strictly with pulling, and the harness should be removed promptly when the workout is finished. As mentioned earlier, in the off-season, beginners should run behind their dogs instead of bikejor, rollerjor, etc., until they feel comfortable controlling their dog. Canicross is the suggested starting point while learning because it affords the greatest control and stability.

If Nothing Seems to Work...

Not all dogs will become proficient at skijoring. A certain amount of confidence and drive is required from a dog to pull in the harness, which to some extent is genetically determined. If you've tried these recommendations without success, especially those involving training with other dogs, you should let your dog return to being a loving pet. When you're ready to purchase another dog, consider a breed with natural pulling inclinations and then do as much research as possible before making a purchase. In the meantime, join a club, watch some races and mingle with a fantastic group of people who enjoy dogs and the outdoors.

Attitude, Consistency, Repetition... Success

Finally, remember to always have a positive attitude when working with your dog. If she doesn't grasp the concept of pulling quickly, assume it's your fault and try again next time with renewed enthusiasm. Attitude, consistency and repetition are the keys to success. Like learning to ride a bike, the experience can be difficult until that one magical moment—then it becomes a skill never forgotten.

CHAPTER FOUR

The Commands

It is not necessary for you and your dog to know all of the commands before skijoring for the first time. If you've read through the safety and basic pulling tips described earlier, you are ready to hit the trail. Skijor commands make the sport more enjoyable but can be learned gradually over a season or two. Our advice is to have fun and learn the commands as you go.

Remember to keep your command training sessions positive and short (10 to 15 minutes), and never lose your temper. The most important skijoring virtue is patience. If your dog isn't learning a command or performing up to expectations, assess the situation from your dog's perspective and try again next training session. One of the axioms of dog training: Whenever your dog makes a mistake, assume it is your fault. This is important because accepting responsibility for a mistake encourages you to remain calm and respond logically. Believe it and act accordingly, and you will end up with a well-trained dog.

Note: Commands are indicated throughout this text in capital letters, as in LET'S GO.

We will assume that your dog already understands and responds to basic commands such as SIT/STAY, NO, DOWN, COME and so forth. If not, we recommend basic obedience training prior to embarking on skijor training. There are many excellent texts available, several of which are listed in the Suggested Reading section. Your community probably offers obedience training courses for both puppies and older dogs. Your initial skijoring experiences will be more enjoyable if your dog is comfortable responding to your basic commands.

Basic Commands

Make sure you understand the skijor commands before teaching them to your dog. Almost everyone confuses GEE (turn right) and HAW (turn left) at least once during his or her first skijoring season. Don't be surprised when you confuse these commands, but recognize that each time you do, your dog will be confused as well.

Speak clearly, with adequate volume, so your dog understands the command. Use inflection to throw your voice and deliver GOOD DOG reinforcements with abundant enthusiasm. When your dog's actions need to be corrected, shout NO loudly and in as low a tone as possible. As a rule, use commands—and words in general—sparingly while skijoring with your dog. The less you talk, the higher the probability your dog will respond when given a command. For example, if your dog is out front pulling like Balto delivering serum to Nome, say GOOD DOG once and then let her focus on doing her job.

Be consistent with your training. Encourage family members to use the same commands and always follow through on any commands that are given. For example, if you ask your dog to avoid stopping at a favorite tree by saying ON BY, do not allow your dog to stop at the tree. If you do—even once—your dog will likely question your leadership and test your resolve in the future, similar to the way a child pushes the envelope of acceptable behavior with his or her parents. Dogs are pack animals and understand hierarchy—you must be a consistent and firm team leader to earn their respect and achieve the desired response.

Use praise as a reward when your dog responds appropriately to commands. See "To Treat or Not to Treat?" for more on this subject.

We suggest teaching the skijoring commands first without skis; this simplifies the process and allows you to focus on the commands. Adding skis to the equation becomes straightforward once you and your dog understand the commands.

Try viewing your training adventures as a one-act play, with you as the director! You know the outcome, or at least the desired

TO TREAT OR NOT TO TREAT?

Providing water is a must. As for treats, there are two schools of thought:

1. Treats are an integral part of training, encouraging and rewarding a dog or

2. Treats are overused and are actually an impediment to the bond between you and your dog.

This debate is beyond the scope of this text and will not be *treated* here! You should continue with what has worked for you in the past, since there is nothing about skijoring that should alter the training and obedience relationship that you have established with your dog.

If you elect to use treats as part of your training regimen, consider these guidelines. Give your dog a treat at the conclusion of your training session or skijoring outing for a job well done. Treating at the conclusion of a session is preferred for several reasons:

1. It is best to have your dog respond to your commands based on your relationship of trust and respect, rather than on anticipation of a treat. Occasions may arise when an immediate response to a command is required, but there is not an opportunity to offer a treat. For example, on the trail you'll have ski poles and gloves to remove before unzipping your jacket pocket to remove treats.

2. If treated regularly, your dog will expect treats regularly and will be disappointed if your pocket is empty.

3. If you're planning to race and want to simulate race conditions, don't treat your dog until after your skijoring session is completed. You'll be too busy during a race to provide treats for your dog.

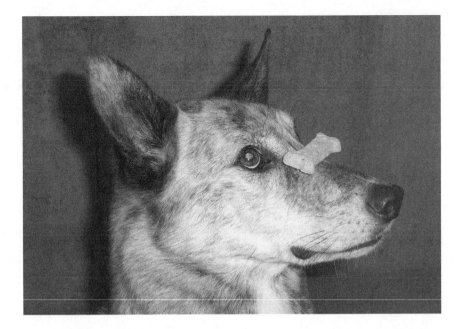

outcome, and you're in charge of the script, lights, sound. . . . even costumes. The point here is to control as many variables and outside influences as possible, just as in a production at your local theatre. Make the most of it by knowing exactly what you want to achieve and by writing your script to make it clear to your dog. The script must stay the same each time—routine and repetition are key. But remember, it's one-act, so keep it short and don't

THE COMMANDS	
Command	*Meaning*
LET'S GO (or HIKE)	Start
WHOA (pronounced "woe," not "woe-uh")	Stop
ON BY	Pass without slowing
GEE (pronounced "g")	Turn right
HAW	Turn left
EASY	Slow down
LINE OUT	Tighten towline
COME AROUND	Turn 180 degrees
GEE OVER	Move to right
HAW OVER	Move to left

THOR

An understanding of commands helps one derive maximum enjoyment from skijoring. Commands help you maintain control and allow skijorer and dog to work as a team. This makes the entire skijoring process safer and easier, from starting down the trail to avoiding obstacles to stopping to undo a tangle. Commands also establish you as the team leader (or alpha dog), providing structure and discipline so that your dog understands who's running the show.

Commands also promote trail etiquette and protect other trail users from unwanted advances from your dog. Consistent use of the commands helps reinforce the appropriate response from your dog.

SPOT

While not always easy, I do acknowledge that commands play an important role in the skijoring partnership. They certainly help keep my human partner under control and can help keep him from becoming injured. After all, he's nowhere near as adept on trails as I am. Commands also provide the structure that humans seem to need and let him feel that he's in charge.

Commands help us go as fast as we can, given the limitations of my human partner. They also protect other trail users by helping prevent "my main man" from having an unsightly wipeout right in front of other dogs and their humans.

However, the strongest case for commands lies in the fact that they eliminate much of that extraneous chatter so common to human discourse—all those unnecessary conjunctions, pronouns, modifiers and the like. Ah, there is something so refreshing about the simplicity of the commands. While I might not always agree with their intent (as in ON BY when there's a delectable squirrel just begging for a visit), I always appreciate how it's being said and thus respond with the appropriate level of deference to reinforce Thor's behavior.

force your cast to repeat it ad nauseam. Dogs' attention spans are short, like those of children (and many of today's adults). Ten or fifteen minutes of training per day is probably enough for most dogs, since you want them to view this as a fun, playful activity.

Set your dog up for a successful outcome. Dog training is most effective when variables are controlled by the trainer. For example, if you're teaching your dog to GEE (turn right), choose a trail that has only 90-degree right turns. If you're having a problem with your dog stopping to visit other dogs while skijoring, have your neighbor and his dog meet you on the trail at a designated place so you can make a correction. Keep alert to your dog's responses as he learns commands; control your movements so that you never run into him. And always have adequate fresh water on hand for your canine companion.

LET'S GO (or HIKE)

How many times have you heard the shout of "Mush" in a sled dog movie as a fur-clad musher sets off down a blustery trail? According to the film industry, "Mush" is the command of choice for sled dog drivers and is used to start a dog team running or press to climatic victory at the finish line. Interestingly, "Mush" is not used in either sled driving or skijoring; instead, both skijorers and mushers use LET'S GO or HIKE to command their teams forward.

You're probably wondering why there are two options for this command. Though their exact origins are unclear, both versions are currently popular and either one will suffice. We prefer LET'S GO because the command works well for a variety of activities: for example, to begin a walk or run. Saying HIKE in these situations may sound peculiar to those not familiar with dog-powered sports.

The command HIKE also has its ardent supporters. Because it's only one syllable, it's faster to say and probably simpler for a dog to learn and remember. Additionally, HIKE is easier to call out when your lips are cold in winter.

Either choice will be effective, but remember you can choose only one. In any event, avoid using words such as okay, which are frequently used in other contexts and are not exclusively associated with skijoring, canicross or bikejoring. For simplicity, we'll use LET'S GO in the discussion below.

Command Uses for LET'S GO

▸ To start your dog moving forward on the trail

▸ To encourage your dog to pick up the pace towards the end of a training run or race

▸ To encourage your dog to speed up after a pass

Training Recommendations: Off Skis

First, we recommend reviewing the "Teaching Your Dog to Pull" section in Chapter 3. Start training by giving your dog the LET'S GO command whenever you move forward with your dog, whether it's walking, running, inline skating or any other activity. As soon as your dog responds appropriately, say GOOD DOG. If your dog does not move forward, say NO, then move forward while simultaneously giving your dog a forward tug on the collar. As soon as your dog starts moving forward, say LET'S GO again and GOOD DOG. By integrating LET'S GO into your daily routine, your dog will quickly learn the command.

Training Recommendations: On Skis

Every dog owner knows that dogs instinctively love to chase practically everything that moves, including other dogs, small game and people. On skis you can take advantage of this instinct by having another skijorer head down the trail ahead of you while you hold your dog back by snowplowing.

After the skijorer is about 50 yards down the trail and when your dog's enthusiasm has peaked, straighten your skis out and give the command LET'S GO. As soon as your dog begins pulling, give her an enthusiastic GOOD DOG and help her attain some speed by skiing smoothly behind her. Keep the towline taut so she can become accustomed to the feel of pulling in the harness. You

can then repeat this procedure another time or two. You'll find that having another skijor team up the trail works best, but a skier will suffice if a team isn't available, especially if your dog knows the skier.

WHOA

At this point you may be wondering why the command WHOA is in the skijoring vernacular. If you've had a successful first outing or two with your dog, you probably can't imagine why you'd want to stop—you simply were having too much fun. On the other hand, if you've had difficulty teaching your dog to pull, you're more than likely questioning the logic behind giving your dog yet another reason to stop!

Teaching your dog to stop on command is important for reasons of safety and convenience. Mushers use a brake as well as verbal commands to stop their teams on the trail. In addition, they can employ a snow hook to hold their sled in place while they tend to their team. Although skijorers cannot use these pieces of equipment, it is possible to effectively control a skijor team with voice commands and ski braking technique alone. An experienced skijorer can run up to three dogs at once, assuming the dogs are well trained and the trail is safe. Beginning skijorers should always start with one dog.

Command Uses for WHOA

- To end your skijoring run

- To avoid dangerous situations such as motor vehicle crossings, unsafe ice or steep descents

- To stop for a tangled line or to check your dog's feet

- To stop for trail hazards that could damage your dog's feet or your skis

- To stop to give your dog a snack or water

Training Recommendations: Off Skis

Incorporate WHOA into your daily routine with your dog. For example, when you stop at an intersection during a walk, give a crisp, backward tug on your dog's leash and say WHOA. When he stops in his tracks, say GOOD DOG. If he doesn't stop, or if he continues to pull against the leash, say NO firmly, repeat the command and procedure, then give him positive reinforcement when he does. You might try having him sit as well. Doing so will increase your control of the situation when you don skis for the first time. In summary, do not allow any forward movement (including your own) after you've given the command.

Training Recommendations: On Skis

Teaching your dog WHOA on skis is more challenging. Unless you are a proficient skier, we recommend starting training while walking. Assuming you are comfortable on your skis, apply the same training procedure as outlined above, using the snowplow or hockey stop (sideways stop using both skis) to halt your dog's forward motion. It's important that the stop is quick, so practice the command while skijoring on a trail that is firm but not hard packed or icy. Remember that WHOA is the command for stopping, not slowing down, which is the EASY command.

Notes:

- If you have been using STOP or some other command for halting your dog, continue using the command unless it's phonetically similar to the other skijoring commands.

- After stopping your dog, use the LET'S GO or HIKE command to start again.

MURPHY'S LAW APPLIED TO SKIJORING

We must digress here for a discussion of Murphy's Law as applied to skijoring and related activities. You probably already know the basic tenet of Murphy's Law—"Anything that *can* go wrong, *will* go wrong, and at the most inopportune time." The authors firmly believe that careful training and preparation are powerful allies in dealing with the unpredictable aspects of skijoring (or should we say predictable unpredictability of skijoring?). However, there will be times when Murphy's Law imposes itself regardless of your Herculean efforts. At such times it is helpful to recognize what is occurring, deal with it as best you can, and move forward. Murphy must have been a skijorer!

Our hope is that you might recognize one or more of these Murphy scenarios when they happen to you, and that you'll A) not take it personally—Murphy does not discriminate—and B) laugh heartily.

Skijoring has required several modifications and extensions to these important scientific principles:

Murphy's Law: Commands

If your dog only understands one command, you will need to use a second, different command. For example, if your dog understands GEE, you'll need HAW. If your dog understands two commands, you will need a third. If your dog understands three commands, a fourth will be necessary. Readers with mathematical training may discern a trend in this data.

Corollary 1

You will not remember the commands that your dog has learned.

Corollary 2

Your dog will not remember the commands that you have learned.

Corollary 3

When it comes to GEE and HAW, you may not even remember the commands that you *thought* you had learned. When in doubt, trust your dog.

ON BY

ON BY is a key command to know once you and your dog are in motion and making tracks. It can be vital on trails that are heavily used by other skijorers, skiers, hikers and cyclists. And it is

useful when you and your dog have the trail to yourself, since there are many natural distractions that can pop up with no warning. Knowing this command can help you avoid the frustration of having your dog continually stopping to greet other dogs and skiers on the trail. It can minimize your need to pry your dog away from the trailside tree that is a local scent post hotspot. It can also prevent being yanked sideways into the woods on an unscheduled pursuit of an audacious chipmunk.

Note: Some skijorers use the command STRAIGHT AHEAD as a substitute for ON BY in many situations. Obedience commands such as LEAVE IT can also be used.

As you might expect, ON BY can be difficult for some dogs to grasp because it runs counter to their natural inclinations to investigate, chase, etc. This only heightens the importance of this command, so have patience with your dog as he learns ON BY.

Command Uses for ON BY

- ▸ To pass an object or distraction without slowing down

- ▸ To continue straight ahead, past that enticing scent post

- ▸ To continue straight ahead, past a turn that is normally taken

- ▸ To ignore the bunny or squirrel that crossed the trail ahead and is now dashing through the woods

- ▸ To pass by without stopping for another dog or skijor team encountered on the trail

- ▸ To continue past pedestrians on the trail

Training Recommendations: Off Skis

ON BY is another command that you can use in your daily routine. In fact, this command is easiest to learn off skis. When on a walk, use ON BY to encourage your dog to bypass distractions such as those listed above.

When a distraction slows or stops your dog's forward progress, say NO. Then, give your dog's leash a quick tug forward while saying ON BY. It's also important for you to continue moving forward at this point. When your dog resumes his forward progress, say GOOD DOG to reinforce the appropriate behavior. Repeat this process and your dog will soon understand what is expected of him.

Once your dog seems to understand this command, introduce selected distractions to test and reinforce the proper response. For example, take your dog past his favorite scent post or tree and make sure he follows your ON BY command. Try placing your dog's favorite squeeze toy on the trail, and come past the object to reinforce ON BY. Or, have a person familiar to your dog appear, perhaps with a dog if possible. This may be quite tempting for an ON BY apprentice, so postpone this exercise until your dog seems ready for the test and be sure to either intervene or praise immediately, as appropriate. For extra credit, try ON BY to override your dog's natural inclination to turn into your driveway.

Training Recommendations: On Skis

As mentioned, try teaching your dog ON BY on foot before attempting on skis. When skiing, it is more difficult to maneuver and maintain balance if your dog bolts off trail. Additionally, delivering a correction is much less effective with a towline and harness than with a leash and collar.

If your dog fails to heed your ON BY command, immediately say NO, then ON BY as you ski around your dog, grab the line and pull him forward. As soon as he resumes his forward motion, say GOOD DOG. Remember to avoid running into your dog from behind. The biggest change introduced by skis is your additional speed, so be prepared to stop quickly or ski around your dog if necessary.

Note:

▸ Once your dog has learned this command, you'll want to say it as early as possible when presented with a distraction. ON BY is much more effective if you can give the command as the bunny starts to run across the trail, instead of after your dog has seen the bunny run in front and into the woods. If your dog hears this command early on, you can help him manage his natural adrenaline surge by reminding him of your desire to proceed ahead. Indeed, waiting until late in the distraction cycle could be perceived by your dog as an invitation to indulge, that perhaps in this particular case it is okay to have an impromptu break. Remove any doubt in your dog's mind by saying ON BY at the appropriate time.

GEE/HAW

GEE/HAW becomes an important pair of commands once you and your dog are in motion, especially if you need to change direction. GEE means right, and HAW means left. It's a relatively easy command set to teach your dog, and in fact the most difficult aspect of GEE/HAW might be teaching yourself. Many skijorers will admit to being frustrated at least once by their inability to remember which direction corresponds to

Gee

Haw

GEE or HAW. Few things on the trail are as frustrating as coming up to that right turn, and then being perplexed by your dog's insistence on turning left when you scream out HAW! when you mean GEE. In any case, we are stuck with these commands so it is imperative that we learn them and try hard not to mix them up. If it takes writing an "H" on your left glove and a "G" on your right, then do just that (and know that you will have plenty of company). You and your dog will both be grateful.

On the flip side, you must also be 100% consistent regarding your dog's response to these commands. Never, ever, not even once, should you permit your dog to turn the wrong way when issuing a command. As in all aspects of obedience training, dogs thrive on consistency, both in terms of your performance and in terms of your expectations. When your dog turns the wrong way, you must stop, repeat the command and get the dog to turn the correct direction, and then praise the dog. It is pretty obvious by now why you must thoroughly understand GEE/HAW before expecting your dog to learn them.

Command Uses for GEE/HAW

- ▸ To make a right or left turn

- ▸ To guide your dog when on a meandering or poorly defined route

- ▸ To combine with the COME AROUND command

- ▸ To combine with the OVER command, as in GEE OVER

Training Recommendations: Off Skis

GEE/HAW is another command set that can be incorporated into your daily routine with your dog. When you're out on a walk with your dog, simply say GEE shortly before a right turn and HAW before a left turn. Give your dog some assistance with a tug on the collar in the correct direction as you say the command. Immediately after your dog completes the turn, say GOOD DOG. Repeating this process over time yields success for the vast majority of dogs.

More structured training can be accomplished by finding a sidewalk or trail that turns a full 90 degrees in one direction only.

Since your dog is limited to turning in one direction, you can easily set your dog up for success and positive reinforcement.

As you approach a single direction turn, for example a right turn, say GEE shortly before your dog enters the turn and GOOD DOG upon completion. Repeat the same procedure for HAW. Try a "T" intersection when you feel your dog understands both GEE and HAW. Be sure to assist your dog by tugging her collar in the appropriate direction the first few times.

Another foolproof technique for teaching GEE and HAW is to have a friend walk down the trail in front of you and your dog, perhaps 25 or 30 feet ahead. The impact of this exercise is enhanced if your friend has a dog with her. Have your friend make a turn in the correct direction, at a specified location. Your dog will naturally want to follow. Just before you reach the turn location, deliver the GEE or HAW command, depending on turning direction. Once your dog makes the correct turn, reward her with praise. As with all commands, repetition is the key to learning and retention.

A potential mishap, also predicted by Murphy, is the inevitable wrong turn caused by telling your dog to turn right when you want to turn left (or vice versa).

Wrong Turn
BOWSER

I was pretty jazzed when Helga took up this new running/skiing thing last year, even though she's no longer a spring chicken. By the way, those spring chickens can be tasty! Anyway, so here we were, cruising along, and Helga sings out HAW! So I head toward what humans also call "left" when all of sudden she pulls hard and barks GEE! Okay, so learn your commands, baby. Or are we just fickle today? I know what they say about not being able to teach an old human new tricks, but this is ridiculous.

GEE and HAW are used because they're simple, one-syllable words that are easy for humans to differentiate. I guess humans do all right overall, considering they can't hear or smell worth a Milkbone. Never understood why they insist on rearing up and standing on their hind legs all the time, though. Not a very stable proposition for travel. Every dog worth his flea collar knows that. Anyway, I was impressed when Helga finally broke down and painted an "H" on one of her paws and a "G" on the other. I don't have to correct her nearly as often.

Training Recommendations: On Skis

GEE/HAW is another command set that you can teach much more effectively off skis, so we recommend starting there. Once both you and your dog are adept with the command, add skis and remember to say the command further ahead of the turn to compensate for the increased speed on skis versus on foot. Be aware that your dog will be able to corner and change direction more rapidly than you can on your skis.

Notes:

- ▶ When teaching this command in a structured setting, you should focus on learning one direction first. Add the opposite direction after both you and your dog are proficient at executing turns in the first direction.

- ▶ Repetition is the key to learning and retention. This means over multiple sessions, not on a single day. Remember the 15-minute rule for structured training, i.e. don't exceed 15 minutes per day of focused training with your dog.

Wrong Turn

HELGA

Sometimes there just isn't much time for careful thought and planning when skijoring. Just the other day, Bowser and I were cruising along on a new trail, when we came up to a fork. Hmm, the snow looks much better to the right; let's go that way. What's the command for right again? Let's see, "H" comes after "G," must be HAW. I need to yell right now; it's coming up fast. HAW! Rats, Bowser is heading left. I must've messed up! Okay then: GEE! Now Bowser is looking back at me like I'm a discarded chew toy. GEE again. There, that's better. Now we're turning right.

Sorry about that, good buddy. Not sure why we can't just go with LEFT and RIGHT, or even PORT and STARBOARD. Guess I know the answer to that one: GEE and HAW are used because they're one-syllable words that are simple for dogs to differentiate, and also because they're easy to say even when your lips are cold. Maybe I'll just capitulate and print a big H and G on my respective skijoring gloves. I won't let Bowser see, lest I suffer a further reduction in credibility in his eyes.

- Be sure your dog understands that GEE/HAW means to turn a specific direction, not just turn any which way. Don't be premature in presenting the diploma for this one; dogs sometimes interpret GEE/HAW as "change direction" without clearly understanding which direction to go. It's also possible for dogs to regress, so be patient and over time your dog will master this command.

EASY

EASY is a great command for those times when you are moving rapidly with your dog and need to lose momentum. Heading downhill on a steep slope is a classic example—it's akin to asking your dog to gently apply the brakes or downshift to avoid becoming a runaway train barreling down a canyon. Your dog will learn to back off slightly upon hearing this command, whether on a downhill slope or flat terrain. EASY allows you to maintain control by managing your speed, thus reducing the chance of a crash or injury from running too fast. EASY is also a useful command when you're approaching a stop or turn on the trail.

Command Uses for EASY

- To reduce your rate of speed
- To reduce the pulling force being applied by your dog
- To get your dog to back off slightly, for example when descending a hill or making a sharp turn
- To maneuver through sections of trail in poor condition
- To keep your dog from running too fast early in a race ("blowing up," in racing terms)

Training Recommendations: Off Skis

When in motion with your dog, say EASY while applying gentle yet firm tension to the towline or leash, so that your dog feels the increased resistance. Pull too hard and your dog may stop, confusing the request with the WHOA command. With the correct amount of tension and repetition, your dog should soon understand the command, and you will feel less forward force on the line. You should then adjust your speed accordingly, so that your dog can modify her tempo and not continue to slow down, unless further deceleration is required. Be sure to give your dog positive reinforcement when she responds appropriately.

Training Recommendations: On Skis

EASY truly is one of the easier commands for your dog to learn. The biggest change when adding skis is that you'll be generating backward resistance by snowplowing or pole dragging to help signal your dog. Anticipation is key—you'll want the speed reduction from EASY to occur when needed, *not* after the challenging section of trail has been completed.

Notes:

▸ When teaching this command, make sure your backward pulling force is distinguishable from WHOA.

▸ EASY is preferred over SLOW or SLOW DOWN, since both sound similar to WHOA or even NO.

▸ Use a softer or calming voice for EASY, and stretch the syllables out (EEA-SY).

LINE OUT

The LINE OUT command simply tells your dog to pull the towline taut while standing. Your dog should learn to keep the line taut until you are ready to start moving (which, of course, you would initiate by saying LET'S GO).

LINE OUT is useful when starting out on the trail; it requires the dog or dogs to move away from the skijorer and lean into the harness in anticipation of the start. This prepares the dog for what is to come next and keeps the line from interfering with your skis and poles as you prepare to start.

Dogs behave differently at the start of a skijoring outing. Some dogs are hyper and lunge into the harness, while others act reserved or even sedated. If your dog is more relaxed, you might try training your dog to sit at the end of the line as you prepare for the start. Because the main objective is keeping the dog and line away from you, a SIT and STAY command can be an effective substitute for LINE OUT.

Command Uses for LINE OUT

- ▸ To pull the towline tight, and keep it tight

- ▸ To signal to your dog that departure is close at hand

- ▸ To prepare for starting out, either initially or after stopping on the trail

- ▸ To encourage your dog to lean into the harness and apply steady forward pulling force

- ▸ To point your dog in the correct direction

- ▸ To keep your dog from circling around and getting tangled up

Training Recommendations: Off Skis

LINE OUT can be effectively taught by attaching your dog's towline to a fixed object such as a tree or car bumper. After securing the towline, pull your dog forward while saying LINE OUT until your dog is leaning forward and the towline is tight. Once your dog is in the LINE OUT position, say GOOD DOG to reinforce the behavior. If your dog does not maintain the LINE OUT position, say NO, then LINE OUT again as you return your dog to the proper position. With time your dog will maintain LINE OUT, even as you circle around him. This method allows you to teach LINE OUT without a second person.

An alternate way to teach LINE OUT is to have a friend help you with this command by pulling your dog forward by the collar as you say LINE OUT. Once the line is taut and you feel steady tension on the line, praise your dog. Instruct your friend to hold your dog in this position for five to ten seconds the first few times. Have your friend return your dog to the LINE OUT position (along with another LINE OUT command from you) if your dog relaxes or begins to move around. However, realize that an experienced dog will soon expect a LET'S GO command after LINE OUT, so don't keep your dog in LINE OUT too long. LINE OUT training becomes easier as your dog develops an association between LINE OUT and LET'S GO.

Training Recommendations: On Skis

When adding skis to this command, you'll need to offset your dog's forward lean as you're fastening ski bindings and making final preparations for starting out. A snowplow position, with your weight on the inside edges of your skis, is best for providing the required equal and opposite force. Your dog should understand the difference between leaning forward just enough to produce a taut line, and actually starting to pull. You don't want the latter—this shouldn't happen until your dog hears LET'S GO. If your dog doesn't LINE OUT, try lightly nudging him with the basket of your ski pole. Or place your dog in a SIT/STAY before putting on your skis.

Notes:

▸ When teaching this command, keep in mind that you are essentially telling your dog "Hey, we're ready to hit the trail." Ideally, your dog will be extremely focused on looking ahead, in anticipation of every dog's favorite command, LET'S GO.

▸ Feel free to use SIT and STAY to keep your dog in a LINE OUT position.

▸ Be prepared to assume a ski tuck position by bending forward at the waist (described in "Safety Tips and Procedures," Chapter 3) if your dog lunges against a slack towline.

COME AROUND

The COME AROUND command is used to get your dog to reverse direction. Most dogs don't back up well in reverse, as they have in innate preference for moving forward. COME AROUND gets them to do an "about face" and move forward in the opposite direction. This is much preferred over trying to get your dog to back up by pulling on the towline, especially if you're wearing skis! This command is very useful if you've fallen and need to collect clothing or equipment, or if you encounter a dead-end trail.

Command Uses for COME AROUND

- ▸ To reverse direction (180-degree turn)

- ▸ To deal with a dead-end trail

- ▸ To reverse direction if a wrong turn is made, or if a problem or obstruction, such as a moose, fallen tree, etc., is encountered on the trail

- ▸ To signal your dog to come back toward you so you can retrieve poles, mittens, or other gear left behind during a fall. In this situation, a second COME AROUND command heads you back in the original direction.

Training Recommendations: Off Skis

COME AROUND is another command that can be worked into your daily routine. For example, whenever you reverse direction during a walk with your dog, say COME AROUND before making the turn. After completing the turn, say GOOD DOG to reinforce the behavior. Soon your dog will execute COME AROUND quickly on command.

For more structured training, place on the trail an object that you can arc around (such as a cone or rock). Walk with your dog towards the object. Immediately after she passes the object, give the COME AROUND command. Smoothly lead her back around the object as you reverse direction. When your dog completes the turn and is headed in the required direction, praise her. Once your dog is comfortable with COME AROUND, you can eliminate the cone or other object from your training.

Training Recommendations: On Skis

When adding skis to this command, there is an increased tendency to become tangled, because you'll need to turn yourself around as well. You may also encounter challenges to your balance while attempting to turn around. Once again, having this command down cold in a non-ski environment will make things easier when you strap on the boards.

Start with a light snowplow and give the EASY command. Snowplow more aggressively as you say WHOA. Say COME AROUND as your dog slows to a stop. At the same time, turn yourself around as you hold the line high and pull your dog towards you. Be patient, since the harness and towline combination is much more effective for the dog pulling you than for you pulling the dog. At this point, you may also need to call your dog towards you using the COME command, followed by LINE OUT. Praise your dog after she is headed in the correct direction. Repeat this process over time, and your dog will gain a solid understanding of this useful command.

Notes:

▸ One of the biggest challenges with this command is to avoid tangles, since your dog will be turning around and reversing direction. Keeping the line high (i.e., above the dog's tail) is the best way to avoid tangles.

▸ When using COME AROUND to reverse direction on a dead-end trail, follow it with a LINE OUT command after you have turned yourself around and are ready to return to the direction you came from. Once your dog has mastered COME AROUND, the LINE OUT command may not be necessary.

▸ If you want your dog to turn in a specific direction when executing COME AROUND, simply preface the command with either GEE or HAW. For example, say HAW COME

AROUND to have your dog start his COME AROUND rotation by turning to the left.

- Once she learns COME AROUND, your dog will turn around more quickly than you can on skis. At a minimum, be prepared for your dog's return to pulling mode before you're completely rotated. Also be ready to assume a ski tuck position by bending forward at the waist (described in "Safety Tips and Procedures," Chapter 3) if your dog lunges against a slack towline.

- Be careful not to inadvertently nick your dog with a ski pole when holding the line high as your dog comes toward you.

- COME AROUND becomes more complex and challenging with multiple dogs.

MURPHY'S LAW: SKIJORING MOTION

Thor is skijoring on a clear day with a two-inch dusting of fresh powder. He and his dogs have already run around the course once and are working smoothly together. His dogs are in great shape, the trail is in excellent condition and the warm up lap has gone well. So he blurts out, "Let's go for warp speed on this one!"

As they round the turn, the dogs accelerate on the gentle downhill stretch. Thor's skis are waxed just right for the conditions, and the team quickly reaches a speed of over 20 mph. With the wind on his face and his dogs perfectly synchronized, Thor glances down to admire his new ski boots and notices that the leg strap on his skijor belt is loose. No problem, he thinks, and reaches down to adjust it.

At that instant, a squirrel darts across the trail, directly in front of the dogs. Armed with knowledge of Murphy's Law, we are able to deduce several Murphy variations relevant to this situation:

Murphy: Motion Extension #1

"The rabbit or squirrel will always cross the trail at that point where you are moving at maximum speed and least able to make adjustments to velocity or direction.

Continued on next page

Continued from previous page

Murphy: Motion Extension #2

"Any disturbance or distraction encountered on the trail will always occur at that instant when you have momentarily directed your attention elsewhere."

Murphy: Motion Extension #3

"The motion of the rabbit or squirrel will always be perpendicular to your direction of travel."

Extension #3 Corollary

"The odds of the rabbit or squirrel running out in front of your dogs, and traveling in the same direction, are approximately equivalent to the odds of winning the New Jersey State Lottery."

Murphy: Motion Extension #4

"The probability of falling or crashing, as well as the apparent severity (e.g., spectator WOW factor) of stated fall or crash, is a function of the number of persons in the immediate vicinity."

With your newly acquired tools and insight, you should be able to predict the outcome of the incident we described. So this may be somewhat anticlimactic: of course the squirrel darted across the trail at a 90-degree angle, at the point where the dogs were at full throttle and at the instant Thor was distracted. His normally well-trained dogs immediately veered off the trail and into the woods, taking Thor along with them. His skis hit the powder snow, slowing him and throwing him off-balance. He was launched from his boards and sailed awkwardly before making a snow angel in the soft powder. Finally, to complete Murphy's prediction, the group of several dozen skiers and onlookers in the nearby parking lot were treated to the spectacle.

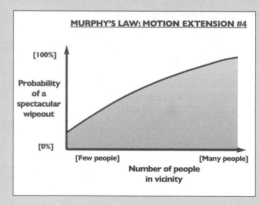

MURPHY'S LAW: MOTION EXTENSION #4

[100%]

Probability of a spectacular wipeout

[0%]

[Few people]   [Many people]

Number of people in vicinity

GEE OVER / HAW OVER

GEE OVER/HAW OVER can be vital commands when encountering oncoming traffic on the trail. This command set enables you to direct your dog to the side of the trail to avoid passing too close to or colliding with oncoming traffic. Similarly, this command set can be useful when there is an obstruction on the trail and you desire to have your dog pass to a specific side of the obstruction. Lacking the GEE OVER/HAW OVER command set, you'll likely be letting your dog choose the route. While this may work in some situations, there are cases where your dog may dart under a branch, taking a natural path of least resistance that is literally a tough act to follow. This command set gives you more control, and thus can also help you avoid minor obstructions such as icy spots on the trail. Finally, these commands are essential when bikejoring or rollerjoring on city streets. In this situation, GEE OVER/HAW OVER can keep your dog close to the curb, or even on the grass if you're traveling on a sidewalk.

Gee Over

Haw Over

Command Uses for GEE OVER/HAW OVER

- ▸ To move to the right or left side of the trail
- ▸ To move over on the trail to let oncoming traffic pass; to allow traffic from behind to pass more easily
- ▸ To avoid trail obstructions such as branches, rocks, glass, bare spots, ice, etc.
- ▸ To move your dog over in preparation for passing another trail user
- ▸ To move your dog closer to the curb when bikejoring or rollerjoring on city streets
- ▸ To pass another skijor team on a specific side

Training Recommendations: Off Skis

GEE OVER/HAW OVER should be taught after your dog has mastered the GEE/HAW command set. Once your dog can respond correctly and consistently to GEE/HAW, she will begin moving in the correct direction upon hearing the first part of this command. You can expedite the learning process by selecting a wider trail for your training sessions. The optimum width is roughly that of a city street; this allows your dog to perceive a definite difference from one side to the other.

Start by walking on one side of the trail. Either side is acceptable—just make sure you're as far as possible to one side of the trail. For example, give a GEE OVER command while walking on the left side of the trail. Pull your dog's leash while you both move to the right side of the trail. When your dog begins moving to the right, praise her. If your dog doesn't respond, repeat the process and emphasize your movement to the right. Begin on the right side of the trail to teach HAW OVER, and use the command to move to the left. When your dog is first learning this command, don't alternate too frequently between GEE OVER and HAW OVER.

Another technique is to find a trail with an occasional meandering turn. Usually, dogs will instinctively take the shortest path from point A to point B, and you can use this natural behavior to your advantage. Look ahead and anticipate when your dog will start moving to the inside of the turn. Give the appropriate command just before your dog starts her shift, and then praise her as she moves to the desired side of the trail. This is an example of setting your dog up for success, because your dog will likely be taking the action anyway and certainly won't mind your praise.

Training Recommendations: On Skis

After you are comfortable off skis with GEE OVER/HAW OVER, you're ready to try the command on skis. The only significant difference is that the leash and collar are replaced with the harness and towline. As mentioned previously, pulling your dog with the towline and harness can be less effective than with a leash/collar combination. This makes it more important to emphasize your movement to the desired side when executing this command.

Notes:

- Mentioned previously, but worth repeating: Make sure you and your dog both understand the basic GEE/HAW commands before attempting GEE OVER/ HAW OVER. This command set becomes much easier with the GEE/HAW foundation.

- If you have one dog that already understands this command, you can run two dogs at dual lead and the one will teach the other by example.

- Using the GEE OVER/HAW OVER command set, you can intervene early in potential distractions to maintain control over your dog. A small game animal up ahead on the trail might inspire you to use GEE OVER/HAW OVER to move to the other side, followed by the ON BY command if necessary.

- Be especially careful when running on roads with motor vehicle traffic. Slow down when encountering traffic so you can stop your team quickly.

Quick Start Guide

Okay, so you've perused the safety section and skijoring commands and want to give skijoring a try. This guide will help you get going on the trail quickly. We assume winter conditions for your maiden voyage. However, you can also try the commands with the simpler, warm-weather alternative to skijoring called canicross, detailed in chapter 9.

Assumptions: Winter XC ski trail, one inexperienced dog and three humans—a skier to chase, a dog holder and a skijorer (you).

1. Try the harness on your dog a time or two at home. Give your dog abundant praise, and let her know this activity will be fun. *Never leave your dog unattended while wearing the harness.*

2. Practice using the rest of your skijoring equipment. Try having a friend pull you on skis to become familiar with

the feel of skijoring, especially at the start. Lean forward a bit to prepare for your dog's initial burst of speed.

3. Choose a trail that is safe, relatively flat and free of sharp turns. Make sure the trail is well defined, and avoid trails with motor vehicle traffic whenever possible.

4. Take water and a snack for your dog, as well as a couple of plastic bags for waste disposal. Bagged pet waste can be carried in an outside mesh pocket on a fanny pack, or double-bagged and carried in a jacket pocket until the next trash receptacle.

5. When you arrive at the trailhead, place your skis where you plan to start, then put your skijor belt on and connect the towline. It is best not to use ski poles on your first outing.

6. Harness your dog and attach the towline to your dog's harness. Choke up on the line so you are closer to your

MURPHY'S LAW: TRIP PLANNING STRATEGY

Two axioms of skijoring are to plan your recreational (i.e., noncompetitive) outing so that A) The final stretch is comparatively relaxing and free from steep ascents, allowing you and your dog to wind down, and B) If there is a wind blowing on a crisp, cold day, one should start out into the wind to ensure that the finish will be with the wind. Hence, it follows that:

1. Left to chance and without your active intervention, the homestretch will involve a grueling ascent up a narrow path that would be considered unacceptable by bighorn sheep. However,

2. Through thoughtful consideration, you can easily select an alternative route. This option will terminate unexpectedly on a trail that has been closed and is not maintained, requiring the skijoring party to trudge through two miles of unbroken trail.

3. Your finish will most likely be into a stiff breeze. Your attempt to thwart this outcome by carefully planning your route and starting out into the wind as described above will be rewarded. However, this reward will be a time-delayed, 180 degree shift in wind direction. This wind shift will become noticeable at precisely that point at which you reverse direction and begin your return to the starting point. Thus, you will have the pleasure of skiing into the wind during your entire outing.

dog for control purposes. *Do not* loop the towline around your hands, fingers, etc.

7. Have your helper lead your dog to the trail so you can put your skis on. The helper should then hold your dog forward, keeping the towline taut. Give your dog some comforting words of encouragement.

8. At this point, your "chasee" skier should be ready to go. Have her head up the trail while calling your dog by name. Your dog should become excited to chase the skier.

9. When the skier is about 40 yards up the trail, say LET'S GO and begin moving forward with your dog. Your helper can assist by pulling your dog forward by the collar. If your dog responds by moving forward, immediately say GOOD DOG and then help her attain some speed by skiing smoothly behind her. Keep the towline taut so she can feel the tension against the harness.

10. Congratulations—you're underway! You can work on commands as necessary but don't overdo it. After LET'S GO, WHOA is the most important command.

10 Tenets of Skijor Training

- ▸ Always remain positive.
- ▸ Keep your training sessions short and fun for your dog.
- ▸ Have plenty of water on hand, and adequate treats (if used).
- ▸ If your dog makes a mistake, assume it's your fault. Your dog wants to please you but doesn't understand how.
- ▸ Enthusiastically reward your dog with praise when she starts pulling.
- ▸ Use words sparingly so your dog listens to you when you do speak.
- ▸ Control as many variables as possible during a run to set your dog up for success.
- ▸ Do not run into your dog from behind.
- ▸ Be consistent in your attitude, commands and routine.
- ▸ Remember that repetition in training is almost always effective but takes time and patience.

SKI SPOT RUN

CHAPTER FIVE

The Dogs

I'll See You On the Trail

I remember when I brought you home, the world amazed you so;
We'd play for hours, you'd chew and run, more energy than I will know.
Not yet wise, but eager? Always! And ready for LET'S GO!
Distracted when squirrels would catch your eye, you'd chase them in the snow.
Let's go and meet the trail!

At 3 years old, you pulled with force yet heeded my command,
Up and down the hills all day; you'd whine for more—I could barely stand.
You were flexible and quick to forgive, when the run didn't go as planned;
Our bond grew stronger and as a team, we challenged ourselves and the land.
You'll pull me to the trail!

By 9 you'd slowed but rationed your strength, jumped less and ran more straight,
Always my companion and trusted friend, like skipper and first mate.
Some say the canine soul is on a higher plane—it has no room for hate;
Anticipating commands before I could ask, and still maintaining your gait.
Let's keep on skiing the trail!

At 13 the glow remained, though I could see it hurt to run,
One look at your harness and your tail would wag—still yearning for more fun.
I wonder if you reminisced, of our days in snow, rain, and sun?
Your gray head on my lap and twinkle in your eye, said you weren't yet done.
I'll carry you to the trail.

Now I ski the trail alone; you're at peace in my woods out back,
As though I'm only partly here, since half our team I lack.
But wait—who's that up front—pulling with your usual knack?
A backward glance from your youthful face, saying, "Let me take up the slack!"
I still see you on the trail.

So far, we've focused on skijoring: the sport, the basic technique and the most important commands. We certainly haven't intended to slight the other critical part of the skijoring equation—your dog! We simply needed to set the stage before delving into the details of *les chiens* (the canines). The passage above conveys the feeling of kinship, camaraderie and dependence that many skijorers and mushers develop for their dogs. This heightens the importance of understanding the characteristics and needs of various dogs before making a dog purchase decision.

Choosing a Skijor Dog

Anyone who has already tried skijoring, or has experienced dog mushing, can attest to the importance of having a good dog or team of dogs. There are obviously many different levels or definitions of "good," but dissecting the term permits a more constructive discussion. For example, it's useful to distinguish between obedience and performance, since "good" is applicable to both. And these are only two potential categories for comparison. You may want to add others such as "adaptability to cold" or "level of care required" if you're trying to compare basic maintenance issues or frequency of exercise demanded by various breeds.

A few sample definitions are presented below, though you'll want to develop your own interpretations. The point here is that the more specific you are in identifying which characteristics are important to you, the greater your chances of success.

Both categories are important, though the relative importance probably depends on your needs and objectives. The very best dogs are strong in both categories and will quickly impress you with their contribution to your efforts and to your enjoyment of the sport. In fact, it's an axiom that you shouldn't test-drive a top-level dog unless you are serious about acquiring such an animal. It is very tough to go back to the familiar or "second-rate" once you've experienced the best.

That said, there are many dogs out there that may not be destined to win a premier race but can still pro-

SPRINGER
SPANIEL

Category	OBEDIENCE	PERFORMANCE
Definition of "GOOD"	▸ Comes when called ▸ Knows GEE/HAW commands ▸ Tolerates other dogs well ▸ Responds to ON BY	▸ Adequate pulling strength ▸ Speed ▸ Perseverance ▸ Endurance

vide you a thrilling and enjoyable skijoring experience. The challenge is to identify what is most important to you, and either work on those qualities with your existing pet, or seek out those qualities if you decide to acquire a dog. If you already have a dog, this section will help you understand more about her strengths and weaknesses. You can then tailor your approach and training to build on the foundation already provided to you, and to bring out the best in your dog. Remember that you must also live with your skijor dog when you're not skijoring—you'll be happiest with a dog breed and personality that are in line with your expectations for all-around pet ownership.

If you plan to acquire a dog, this analysis will help you decide which characteristics are most important. One caveat: the following generalizations are based on experience and are reliable in the aggregate. However, as you might expect, dogs are generally not aware of the aggregate; each dog has a unique personality. These

Dog Breeds
HELGA

Keep in mind that you'll probably end up disappointed if you try to make your dog into something she is not. Some breeds have a natural tendency toward certain characteristics, which have been selected and developed over many generations. Pointers were originally bred for pointing, shepherds for herding, sighthounds for chasing, and so on. That's not to say that these dogs can't or don't make excellent skijoring choices; all three breeds have been cross-bred for dog-powered sports. It's just that you should consider the heritage of a particular breed when making your plans. While many things are possible, there are some limits to what you can realistically expect your dog to do.

guidelines are intended to help as you determine what works best for your situation.

Some dogs and dog breeds have trail running and pulling in their veins, owing to their working-dog ancestry. Such dogs are a joy to skijor with and will teach their owners many things while simultaneously delivering top performance. Alaskan huskies, Siberian huskies and Alaskan malamutes are familiar sled dog breeds that one would expect to be at home pulling a skijorer. Breeding is extremely important; the working ancestry can be different from the pet or show dog bloodline. If you're purchasing a puppy, ask to see a dog's parents pulling in the harness for insight into the pup's pulling potential.

The Internet is a great source for more information on dog breeds. Try searching under "dog breeds," "sled dogs" or a particular breed of interest, such as "Siberian husky."

These working dogs are not for everybody, however, and may not be suited to the casual, weekend skijoring enthusiast. One reason is that working breeds tend to require more activity and exercise, having been bred over many generations for this purpose. These breeds may become agitated and unruly if you don't deliver on your end of the agreement (i.e., take them out for frequent exercise). Another

K.H. RAUBUCH

characteristic of working dogs is their strong desire to pull, and to pull hard. This may be fine for your circumstances, but may be a hassle if you are more inclined to casual touring, or if you frequently run with your dog on hard pavement. Concrete or asphalt can rapidly wear a working dog's toenails and pads down to the point of bleeding (see sidebar, Chapter 9, "How NOT to Set Your Bike on Autopilot"). A prong collar or head halter should be used with such dogs on pavement, so they know it is not time to pull.

Note that even outstanding sled dogs accustomed to pulling in a team will sometimes balk at pulling a skijorer. Skijor dogs are required to be leaders, and not all dogs feel confident and willing to pull in front. A dog familiar with running in a sled team may also be startled by a skijorer's skis and poles, as well as the movement, different sounds and heavier load. These challenges can usually be overcome with time and patience. Be sure to "test drive" any adult sled dog on a trail familiar to the dog before buying. To increase the chance of success, have a sled or skijor team run ahead on the trail.

Less obvious, perhaps, are the many golden retrievers, black labs, Irish setters, beagles, poodles and other breeds that are very capable of turning in fine performances on the skijoring trail. In fact, the instincts to pull and to run on a trail are so

LABRADOR
RETRIEVER

THE DOGS

common that most of these breeds and many others can make excellent skijoring dogs. For this reason, we will focus on dog *characteristics,* not on specific breeds. The characteristics listed here are probably a better predictor of skijoring success than a list of breeds, with the exception of sled dogs previously mentioned.

What is the probability of someone competing and doing well in skijoring with a typical household pet? At the very highest levels, you will find yourself surrounded by elite breeds such as greysthers, Scandinavian or Eurohounds, and Alaskan huskies. A greysther is a German shorthaired pointer crossed with a greyhound, while a Scandinavian or Eurohound is an Alaskan husky crossed with a German shorthaired pointer and/or an English shorthaired pointer. Race-bred dogs are the canine equivalent of mating top Olympic athletes, choosing the best offspring for breeding, and then repeating the process over many generations. These dogs are bred by racing kennels dedicated to developing the fastest, strongest and heartiest dogs possible. In elite races, bringing home a trophy probably requires a race-bred dog and an accomplished skier.

But virtually everywhere else, these breeds are not mandatory, and in fact you'll probably observe a plethora of other breeds competing extremely well. And most important is that you'll likely observe that they and their owners are having a grand time.

In summary, if your skijoring goal is primarily recreation-oriented, or recreation along with some racing, your retriever, springer, lab, poodle, setter, beagle and so on, is probably an excellent choice. On the other hand, if you know at the outset that you intend to train and compete frequently, and you are a proficient enough competitor yourself that you will not be viewed as an "anchor" by a high-performance dog, then you should consider a top northern or elite breed. And, if you fall somewhere in between, we'd advise starting out with the household pet that you already own or plan to acquire. Such dogs are generally more tolerant and patient with humans on a steep learning curve!

Check your area to see if there is a local skijoring or mushing club.

GERMAN
SHORTHAIRED
POINTER

Events sponsored by such organizations can be an excellent place to observe dogs in action and talk with people who are knowledgeable about and genuinely love dogs. Clubs sometimes host "fun runs" where you can borrow equipment and try running or skiing behind your dog. It may be worth your while to attend one of these events even if it requires driving some distance; you'll gain an abundance of knowledge on the topic in a very short time.

Jump for the Stars

GINGER

Here we go again, waiting once again for Thor to get his act together. Not sure what the holdup is. We're just standing here wasting time. If we don't take off soon, that squirrel I smell will be in the next county. Man, we only do this trail thing once or twice a week! We don't have time to hang out here, adjusting equipment and trying to get everything just right. What is it with all this gear anyway? Such complexity—I feel sorry for him sometimes. I'm pretty much wash-n-wear, roll-out-and-head-out, but my dude needs his entourage of personal paraphernalia. My fur coat seems as waterproof and breathable as any of his attire. Never understood why they don't just let their fur grow longer to cover their entire body.

Dog Traits Good for Skijoring

General Characteristics. The following traits suggest that your dog might enjoy and excel at skijoring. If your dog

- Enjoys running outdoors
- Stays in front on walks
- Has good stamina and energy
- Likes to please you
- Likes to catch up to people or dogs ahead on the trail
- Has drive and a good attitude
- Is 30 pounds or more (or a rambunctious 20 pounds),

then your dog might be a natural for skijoring. If your dog has displayed any of these traits, she may be just waiting for you to say, LET'S GO!

Gait. The objectives here are smoothness and efficiency of effort. Ideally, there should be minimal up and down movement, side-to-side motion or choppiness. Cross-country skiers will already have an instinctive understanding of this concept; they know that whatever energy they redirect from lateral motion can be harnessed as forward progress. Dogs with a smooth and efficient gate may not

---

Jump for the Stars

THOR

Sometimes dogs are so anxious to get moving that they will begin jumping wildly, almost uncontrollably, in anticipation of the LET'S GO command. It can be an amusing scene: the skijorer is trying to get the dog to sit still or LINE OUT (pull the line taut) while he completes the drill of putting on skis, hooking up skijor belt, and so forth. A normally serene canine can suddenly become the equivalent of a Type A, chain-barking, intolerant personality as you fumble with your equipment. The rare pet that waits patiently and observes while you complete your pretrail routine is either exceptionally well-trained, an advanced geriatric or blessed with an innate understanding of the feeble human condition.

---

even appear to be working very hard, but don't be fooled. The towline is a good indicator— it is tight nearly all the time behind an efficient, hard-working dog.

If you own a dog, you probably already know if she likes to run and if she seems to run with a fluid motion. If your dog appears to struggle when running, you should consult a veterinarian to identify the underlying cause. Sometimes inactive dogs are overweight, and simply shedding a few pounds can improve their gait. If your dog is sedentary, start slowly with your skijoring program. Problems may also be caused by arthritis or some other malady, which can sometimes be controlled by medication.

GOLDEN RETRIEVER

Consult a veterinarian regarding your dog's specific problem before beginning skijoring or before administering any medication. Unlike physical conditioning, which will improve once your dog gets in the skijoring "habit," problems with gait may worsen because they can be indicative of other issues requiring medical attention.

If you are considering buying a dog, try to see him run in harness. Unless you would consider buying a car without a test drive, don't consider acquiring a dog without seeing him in motion. Watch for a fluid motion, the amount of effort that the dog appears to be expending, and the dog's stamina and drive. If possible, join the owner and the dog for a brief run along a trail, where you can observe the dog running for ten minutes or more. If you're unable to see the dog run in harness or on the trail, another way to evaluate gait is to have the dog fetch a ball or run and play with you in the yard. Be creative and remember that your goal is to observe the dog in motion.

Size. While there are no absolute lower or upper limits to a dog's weight for skijoring, the majority of skijoring dogs are 30 pounds or more. And even this statistic is not ironclad; out on the skijor trail there are plenty of dogs that weigh less than 30 pounds. Apparently no one bothered to tell them. Actually, as long as a dog

STANDARD POODLE

likes to run on the trail and can keep the line taut, pulling power is not essential. This helps explain why Helga observed a 20-pound beagle charging by on the trail, skijorer in close pursuit.

At the upper end of the spectrum, large dogs offer advantages in terms of sheer pulling power. Though big dogs may not set course records for speed, they are an excellent choice for pulling a pulk for winter camping, or trotting around a golf course ski trail.

If you already own a dog, there obviously isn't anything you can do to affect his size. No, we would not endorse a program of daily steroids and interaction with professional heavyweight wrestlers. If you skijor with a smaller dog, pay close attention to how your dog responds when pulling on the trail, and take your cues from her performance and attitude. Your dog's smaller size will require you to contribute more effort to the motion equation. It may also make your dog more susceptible to any jerkiness caused by your skiing motion. To reduce the effect your movement has on your smaller dog, ask your equipment supplier for a towline constructed of a thinner gauge bungee: 1/4" or 3/16" diameter, depending on the weight and pulling strength of your dog.

If buying a pup, ask to see the parents or grandparents to estimate the dog's likely adult size. Keep in mind, though, that this is an inexact science, similar to using paw size as an indicator of future growth.

Musculature and structure. The dog should appear fit, with good muscle tone and moderate fat composition. Avoid extremes if possible—for example, very long or short legs, overly musclebound, etc. These characteristics may make for an interesting looking dog, but rarely increase performance. A dog's musculature should be compared to the standard for the breed. Breed photographs, drawings, or paintings can provide a basis for comparison. A benefit of skijoring is that a dog's muscle tone will improve once you begin hitting the trail!

Mature dogs can be masters of efficient operation, substituting experience for raw caloric output. In her younger days, my beloved setter Alta would run nine miles off leash to my one, darting on and off the trail while I jogged prosaically along. Later in her life she became more of an escort, as she conserved momentum and was thus able to continue to run for many years. And patience is a virtue favoring older dogs. An eight-year-old canine is probably less hyper and high-strung, making her more tolerant of any mistakes or delays that occur on the trail.

Age. Chronological age is a factor in a dog's skijoring potential, though its role is not always obvious. Young dogs are more malleable, a sort of clay to be molded into a desired form. Juvenile dogs are likely to provide sheer power and have an energy level that will literally leave you breathless. Older dogs, on the other hand, have well-developed routines, whose modification requires persistence and patience.

If you own an older dog, chronological age may or may not be a reliable predictor of your dog's skijoring potential. If your dog is in good health and enjoys running on the trail, there is really no upper limit that should restrict her participation in skijoring. Older dogs may lack speed and strength but still provide an enjoyable outing. Start slowly when training an older dog by keeping distances short and increasing mileage gradually.

If your dog is less than a year old, there are several factors to consider. At six months and older, you can start acclimating your dog to the harness. This could include trying on the harness, pulling a light object around the yard, or running a short distance in harness. Don't attempt to have your pup do any hard pulling; wait until he is an adult. Always be positive and be sure to quit well before your pup becomes

BERNESE MOUNTAIN DOG

tired. Be considerate of your dog's attention span, which will be short. The goal is to have your dog yearning for more.

If buying a dog, you'll need to decide if you want a puppy or a mature dog. This decision probably has more to do with whether you want to "start from scratch" when training your dog, or hit the ground running. Of course, the decision is also driven to some extent by which dogs are available during your search. Starting with a puppy means that your dog will not be bringing along many "bad habits" that someone else has taught her (so any bad habits will be learned from you!). However, buying a mature dog means you may be better able to view and assess the dog's performance as a skijoring dog prior to the purchase.

Intelligence. A dog of average intelligence can learn to skijor. The most important factor is a dog's understanding of the concept of pulling in front. Dogs with an innate pulling instinct have a head start here; they naturally gravitate to the front. For dogs that lack a strong pulling instinct, intelligence can compensate by making it easier to train them to stay up front and pull. Learning the various skijor commands can be difficult for some dogs, but remember that not all commands are necessary for your dog to skijor. Repetition and patience are the keys to training and can produce impressive results with most dogs.

Attitude. A trump card, since this aspect alone can override virtually any of a dog's characteristics. Ignoring it is risky. A dog's drive, desire to please, confidence, mental toughness and tolerance can make up for physical shortcomings most any day of the week. Unfortunately, the reverse is also true: a dog's bad attitude can negate physical superiority faster than a speeding gravy train.

If you own a dog, you're probably aware of your dog's general approach and attitude, and you can apply this knowledge when taking her on the skijoring trail. You may benefit from spending a few minutes beforehand trying to predict how she will react so you can plan your response. How well did you predict your dog's behavior? And how well did you plan your response?

If acquiring a dog, try to obtain as much knowledge as possible about attitude through observation and inquiry. Chatting with a current or previous owner can provide useful information about the dog's attitude and general character, social skills with humans and

Call it telepathy, or maybe it's just slightly reduced tension in the towline. At any rate, your dog always seems to know when you're momentarily off balance. For whatever reason, a dog will typically choose this as the moment to either accelerate or change direction, sometimes providing unexpected excitement. For example, hitching up your dog and putting on the first ski is usually straightforward, since you have one foot free for balance. The second ski can be interesting, however. When you lean down to tighten the binding on the second ski, be careful. Dogs love to equate this to the water skier's shout of "Hit it!" and may take off down the trail.

other dogs, physical strength and endurance, patience and any other qualities important to you. Ask about and observe the dog's parents or grandparents for important clues regarding these qualities.

It is important to understand dog characteristics, both for the purpose of selecting a dog and understanding your animal as you journey together. It is also instructive to consider how your dog perceives the world. You'll gain insights into training and managing your dog, and you might be intrigued by a different perspective on "ordinary" sights and sounds.

Northern Lights Lupine Choir

To a skijorer or a musher, it is arguably the sweetest sound on earth. That visceral, high-pitched howl emitted by dogs in the wild. A throaty cry that is both haunting and melodious to those that know them well. And a chorus of such voices is clearly to be savored.

The skijorers and mushers had stopped for the evening at a small motel, hoping for a restful night before the big race the following morning. The Northern Lights Motel was right off a rural highway, and consisted of twin buildings on opposite sides of the property with guest vehicles and dog trucks arranged in the center. The establishment was doing a brisk business that snowy evening, with perhaps 40 human guests and 150 dogs checked in for the night.

People and dogs had bedded down for the night, with a majority already drifted into slumber. As one skijorer lay awake contemplating the events of the next morning, she thought she heard the faint sound of a police siren, very far away. Strange, she thought, how a sound like that seems intrusive out here, miles from the nearest village.

Then it started: slowly at first, finally gaining momentum, going from tremulous to confident. First one dog, then two, three, five, then twenty singing their own siren song. Like an enormous piece of machinery that requires effort to be put in motion, the quintessential pack howl does not gear up immediately. Dogs started, broke off and started again with renewed vigor, each time enticing their kennel mates to join in. Within a minute all 150 dogs were eager participants in the project, and the crescendo had reached an intensity that would dwarf the wolf packs of Alaska or the Yukon.

Skijorer and musher alike stirred in their beds, some enjoying the soothing tones, others preferring the sleep from which they had just been summoned. All would agree, though, that this was truly the call of the wild. The question was, how many stanzas could the dogs muster tonight?

As if in answer, the chorus began to taper as dogs dropped out of the refrain in twos or threes. Soon there was just a handful of voices keeping the howl alive, and then only one or two. But these stalwarts were secure in their role as "keepers of the flame," and the howl hung on in their custodial grasp. Eventually another dog chimed in, then another, then several more, and soon the engine was revved up again. Once more it peaked, with the entire parking lot joining in sympathetic symphony, challenging the long-subsided police siren for tonal supremacy.

The cycle continued for several more rounds that evening at the Northern Lights Motel. Eventually the dogs' orchestral appetite was sated, and they let the ghost of the howl move on to another convocation, to work its magic elsewhere. The police siren had acquiesced, wailing in protest as it fled into the distance. The skijorer relaxed and drifted into deep sleep, secure in the knowledge that justice had been done.

CHAPTER SIX

The Equipment

One of the remarkable characteristics of skijoring is its simplicity: it requires minimal equipment. The dog in particular needs very little gear in order to enjoy the sport. However, this means that the equipment that *is* involved becomes very important, especially regarding quality and fit. As with most outdoor and sporting gear, it usually pays to spend the extra few dollars to buy the better or best quality gear and to avoid the cheapo aisle.

Once that initial spark of interest in skijoring has struck, the challenge becomes how to experience the sport for the first time. There are many paths to this goal, ranging from borrowing equipment and/or dog to participating in a seminar or fun run held by a local skijoring or mushing club. The latter events are generally low- or no-cost gatherings provided by helpful volunteers in the interest of promoting increased understanding of dog-powered sports. Whatever route you choose, consider the sagacious advice to try before you buy. For those who haven't tried skiing, many parks and ski areas will allow you to rent skis, boots and poles to sample the cross-country skiing experience before you plunge in and buy ski

Equipment Matters

THOR

Taking the time to obtain good quality equipment and proper fit can make all the difference between a difficult and an exceptional run. And since it's challenging to make modifications on the trail, it's best to spend a couple of extra minutes at the trailhead taking care of any last-minute adjustments. Keep in mind that dogs don't like stopping once they're underway because they don't understand why they're no longer in motion. It's a good idea to learn how your equipment works before hitting the trail, including the best way to put the harness on your dog and how to operate the quick-release mechanism.

BOWSER

There is nothing quite like the feel of a snug-fitting harness. In fact, the human expression "fits like a glove" never made much sense to me. They should really try one of these things on—they would probably change their saying to "fits like a harness." Now that would be a sight to behold: Thor in harness, pulling me on skis—LET'S GO! I wonder how much pulling power I could get out of him?

My vote for second best piece of equipment is the bungee shock cord that connects human to power train (me!). It makes a tremendous difference, as it helps adjust for the fact that humans don't always accelerate that well and can have difficulty maintaining a constant gait.

And regarding adjustments on the trail—humans sometimes have trouble understanding that trails were created for motion, not idle chatter, stationary reflection or stopping to fine-tune equipment. My advice: spend the extra few minutes at the trailhead getting ready, or better yet, do this at home before I've been exposed to the sights, sounds and smells at the trailhead.

equipment. The previous chapter describes what criteria to consider when selecting a dog for skijoring. The following sections detail the key pieces of equipment used in the sport.

The Harness

The most important piece of skijor equipment, at least for the dog, is the harness. This makes it essential that the harness be properly constructed and fitted. Ideally, your dog's harness should fit so well that he doesn't even notice it, that it essentially functions as and becomes a part of him. The harness should cradle the dog and engender confidence. It should feel good to him even when he is pulling hard. Otherwise, the harness can cause a distraction from the skijoring experience. And any distraction is unwelcome, because of the relatively short attention span of most canines. (Au-

X-Back harness

thors' note: Humans have recently been working hard at challenging canines to lay claim to the shorter attention span. Recent human preoccupation with multitasking has significantly narrowed this gap.) The bottom line is that both you and your dog will enjoy skijoring much more if your dog is able to focus on the sport, not on the harness.

The harness fit should be snug and conform to your dog's body. A loose or baggy harness can shift back and forth and cause chafing, especially on dogs with short hair. This shifting can also misalign the pulling forces on the dog.

A rule of thumb is that no moving parts on the dog should contact the harness. For example, the neck piece should not contact the shoulder joint, and the leg straps shouldn't rub the inside of the dog's legs. The tendency of leg straps to rub is a function of harness chest plate length. A chest plate that is too short allows the leg straps to separate before passing an adequate distance through the dog's legs.

Proper harness fit should be gauged when the harness is snugged up from behind while the dog is standing straight. Normally a dog will lean against the force, and this is actually preferred for determining the best fit. If your dog has a thick coat of fur, pull the fur through the neck piece so the harness seats on the dog rather than on the fur.

The harness neck piece or yoke should rest on the part of the dog where the neck intersects the body. This point is below the dog's collar, but above the sternum and forward of the shoulder blades. Once seated, the neck piece should be snug but not tight. Make sure your dog's collar is positioned above the neck piece so

Improper fit: harness too long

Improper fit: harness too short

that it is not trapped underneath when you hit the trail. Since swinging dog tags can be a distraction to your dog, avid skijorers will sometimes use a smaller ring for attaching the tags, or an alternate collar with riveted tags.

When pulling the harness over your dog's head, the ears will tend to pull back. This is acceptable, but the harness should slide over the head relatively easily. Once the neck piece is seated, try placing your index fingers beneath the padding above and below the neck webbing or yoke. If this is difficult, the neck opening is probably too small; conversely, if there's an abundance of space, try a harness with a smaller neck size.

The harness material, not the connecting loop, should end at the base of the dog's tail (or slightly beyond) when snug. The key is to make sure the side straps do not interfere with hind leg movement. Check for binding at the rib cage, and note whether the harness webbing on the back of the dog lies flat when a pulling load is applied to the harness. For example, the "X" on an X-back harness should become taut and form-fitting when the harness is pulled snug. If a stock harness doesn't fit your dog properly, consider having a custom harness made to his individual measurements.

Harness Installation

(All photos by John Sandberg)

Straddle dog and hold with knees or place in SIT/STAY.

Grasp harness chest plate and neck piece separately.

Pull neck piece downward to meet leg straps.

Align neck piece with leg straps to create opening.

Pull harness over dog's head. Chest plate should fall beneath dog's chin.

Pull neck piece and leg straps over collar.

Pull leg straps downward.

Reach through leg strap to grasp dog's leg at knee. Use other hand to hold leg strap.

Bend foot backward at knee and pull leg through strap opening. Move leg in dog's natural range of motion.

Check harness for twisted straps and proper neck piece seating. Picture illustrates proper harness fit.

A good outfitter or dealer will carry numerous harness sizes and will take the time to personally fit your dog. For each neck size there are usually two or three different length/width combinations available. The time spent ensuring that your dog has a high quality, good-fitting harness will pay dividends each and every time you venture out on the trail.

The X-back harness is currently the most common in skijoring and mushing. The X-back is popular because it provides a supportive, glove-like fit, yet doesn't restrict breathing or movement. It also incorporates more webbing material, making it difficult for a dog to back out of. The X-back is easily identified with the two top straps forming an "X" on the top of the dog's back.

Another common harness design is the H-back, in which the straps extend straight back along the length of the dog. This design is sometimes used in distance mushing, although it offers less support than an X-back in the rib and back area.

Avoid walking- or tracking-style harnesses, which can exert too much pressure on the bottom of your dog's neck when skijoring. These harnesses attach midback, rather than at the base of the tail and usually require a very steep leash or line angle to distribute pulling forces evenly.

Regardless of the harness design you choose, be sure to carefully inspect the materials and stitching quality. A good quality harness should come with at least a one-year guarantee on materials and workmanship. A reputable dealer or outfitter should also guarantee the fit of the harness.

The harness webbing material is typically nylon with either open- or closed-cell foam padding. Closed-cell foam is similar to wetsuit material and is preferred for its cushioning qualities and resistance to water absorption. Fleece can be an excellent covering material for closed-cell foam because it rounds the edges of the padding and has a warm, fuzzy feel to the dog. Combining closed-cell foam and fleece will yield optimum comfort and shock absorption for your dog without unnecessary bulk. A harness with bulky padding can limit a dog's freedom of movement by overlapping moving parts of the dog.

Once again brand names are important. Several manufacturers offer high quality fleece that holds its shape and wears well. The only drawback to fleece material is that it tends to absorb water, so avoid fleece if you regularly run your dog in wet conditions. In this case, choose closed-cell foam covered in nylon.

LISA HAAKENSTAD

Harnesses are generally available in two different weights of nylon webbing, usually in a one-inch width. Recreational harnesses often feature the heavier weight, which is more difficult for a dog to chew through. Racers prefer the lighter-weight version, which is more than adequate for everyday use. To illustrate, lightweight webbing has a breaking strength of 1,300 pounds, while an average dog exerts only about 300 pounds of maximum force against a harness. This makes stitch quality and thread type just as important as the webbing material. Look for a boxed stitch pattern (a box with an "X") on webbing joints, and double reinforced stitching on areas that will be subjected to high stress. Heavy-duty polyester thread with ultraviolet (UV) protection is preferred.

Good quality harnesses come with reflective strips as standard equipment. There is a performance difference in both the reflective distance and radius among various manufacturers' reflective products. A material with superior reflective radius will provide improved brightness when viewed from more angles. Choose a harness that incorporates high quality reflective materials such as 3M® brand. It's also important that the harness be reflectorized from the front as well as the sides to maximize reflective radius. Even if you don't plan to run your dog at night, it's best to have reflective strips, just in case you're caught out late or the day turns dark. This advice also applies to skijor lines and belts, covered later in this chapter.

Clean your harness by hand or by machine washing on delicate cycle with a mild detergent. Be sure to rinse thoroughly to eliminate residual soap, and line dry rather than tossing into the dryer. Unless the harness is particularly dirty, frequent washing is unnecessary. However, it is imperative to store the harness in dry, open air when wet so it can dry completely. Washing a harness once a season is usually sufficient to remove the grit and grime that shorten harness life. A good quality harness that is properly cared for will provide many seasons of enjoyment.

Possibly the greatest threat to harness life is chewing. A dog can very quickly chew through even the best nylon material, requiring repair or rendering a harness completely worthless. For this reason, a primary rule is to never leave your dog unattended in harness. A simple tenet is that when the harness is on, the dog is "working," i.e., running on the trail, pulling the skijorer. "Working" is the term from the lexicon of mushing, though to the dog this seems more like play than work. When the run is completed and the dog is no longer working, the harness comes off immediately. In fact, your dog should not run free or play around when in harness. Ideally, your dog should develop a very close association between wearing the harness and pulling up front. The tighter this relationship, the better it is for you, your dog and the harness.

Consistent application of this approach, starting with the harness-breaking period when your dog is first exposed to the harness, will yield optimum results. The term harness-breaking is borrowed from equestrians, though it is hardly an accurate comparison. The

MURPHY'S LAW: THE HARNESS

The dog harness always goes on most quickly when it is either inside-out or up-side-down. Dogs (for whatever reason) are most cooperative when the harness is in one of these two states, and they will facilitate your efforts to speedily deploy it to their torso.

Corollary 1

When you have the harness correctly positioned for putting it on your dog (i.e., right-side up, neckpiece toward front of dog), your dog's excitement will impede your efforts, and it is more difficult to put the harness on the dog.

Corollary 2

Removing an improperly installed harness is not as easy as putting it on improperly, as the dog senses that somehow the skijoring outing is on the verge of being postponed. A dog will resist efforts to remove an improperly installed harness, in inverse proportion to the correctness of installa-

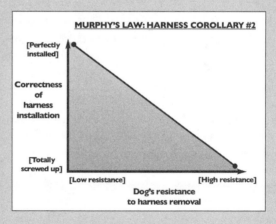

tion. In other words, the more screwed up you've gotten the harness on your dog, the more your dog will resist its removal.

reason is that while horses absolutely loathe their initial contact with the bit, reins and saddle, most dogs are innately programmed with a desire to run on the trail. Hence, the harness-breaking period refers not to breaking the spirit of the dog, but to developing the association between a piece of equipment and a specific activity. It may help to think of it as simply providing rules and structure to what will likely become your dog's very favorite pastime. Your dog may actually view the harness as liberating, since it provides her the freedom to pull.

Keep your dog's first exposures to the harness brief and positive. Try to err on the conservative side and control as many variables (elapsed time, distance traveled, trail type and condition, etc.) as possible. This is especially important when dealing with puppies. At six months, harness work should be limited to very brief pulling episodes. Resist the temptation to continue training longer when things are going well, because you can stay focused longer than your dog can. Ideally you will finish on a positive note, praising and encouraging your dog. This is preferred over ending up three miles from your car with a tired and frustrated dog.

The Belt

Skijor belt with leg straps and stainless steel quick-release

Many recommendations concerning the dog's harness apply equally to the belt worn by the human. Snug fit, comfortable padding, quality material—such characteristics are likely to be prized by pooch and person alike. However, chewing of the belt has been reported to be less of a problem, owing to the reduced stress tolerance of human teeth.

A skijor belt should be light in weight, and feel and function as an extension of the body. In fact, the whole idea is for the belt to "disappear" on the wearer, so take your time when fitting and adjusting the belt to ensure a correct fit. The belt should be wide enough to disperse the dog's pulling force while allowing freedom of movement. The most common belt width is 4". Open-cell foam is preferred over closed-cell foam for its greater flexibility. This enhances comfort for skijorers, who tend to continually shift position, balance and posture (e.g., bend at the waist) while executing different skiing techniques.

When fitting a new belt, start out by wearing it at hip level. Next, experiment to find the "sweet spot" where your center of gravity is located. Experienced skijorers will tend to wear the belt slightly higher, since this position offers more adjustment options for counteracting pulling forces. For example, when a skijorer is pulled forward she can use her legs to offset the force in

Skijor belt front view

Skijor belt side view

the same way a downhill skier adjusts her balance. Counteracting these forces is more difficult when the belt is lower on the body, because in that scenario the skijorer's legs tend to be pulled out from underneath.

When purchasing a belt, select one with leg straps. They help to stabilize the belt and prevent it from riding up on your torso. Leg straps also provide extra support, which you'll appreciate if you need to assume the ski tuck position described earlier. This extra support also keeps the belt from rotating or sliding around on your waist.

Belts are now available with flexible suspension side straps, which move the weight of the bungee closer to the skijorer. When the dog pulls on the line, the force elongates the bungee in the towline as well as the side straps on the belt. The elongation properties of the belt and line can be selected for specific load responses to provide a variable rate of suspension. These innovations absorb both light and heavy shocks against the line and help moderate the speed differential between dog and skijorer. The suspension belt also permits the use of a lighter weight bungee in the towline, resulting in less swing weight and jump rope effect. Tangles are reduced by the recoiling action of the belt and line working in concert. The system works particularly well on hilly courses.

Old-style belts were attached to the towline with a heavy, cumbersome quick-release, commonly referred to as a "panic snap." Newer belts often feature a lighter weight, stainless steel quick-release which is permanently affixed to the belt. The new design prevents the metal hardware from following your dog down the trail upon release. Besides reducing the weight of the belt/towline combination, the lighter snap reduces swing weight, which is especially noticeable in slack line situations.

Newer belts are also available with removable leg straps. This feature is a welcome option for those choosing to wear the belt over running shorts in warmer weather, since it eliminates potential chafing from the leg straps. This can be a plus if you use the belt during the summer for canicross or rollerjoring.

Make sure the belt is equipped with a reflective strip and is constructed of high quality materials and stitching similar to that described for harnesses.

Belt/Towline Connections

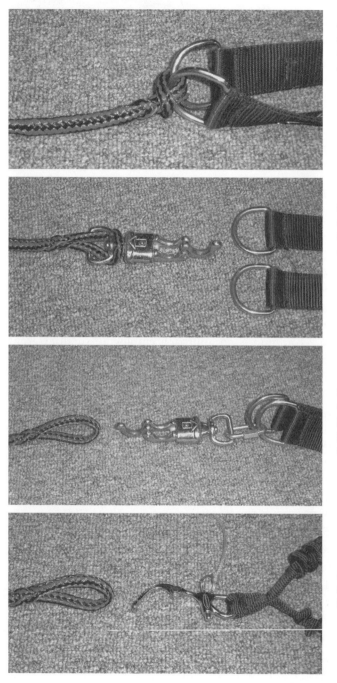

Not recommended—
line connected directly
to belt without quick-
release device

Not recommended—
heavy quick-release
stays with line upon
release

Not recommended—
release arrow on snap
faces wrong direction:
false releases likely to
occur

Recommended—quick-
release remains with
belt upon release

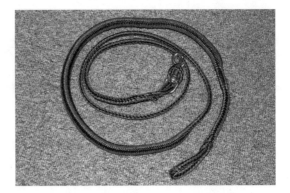

Skijor towline with internal bungee

The Towline

The best quality skijor line is made from polyethylene, rather than polypropylene rope. Polyethylene has a softer, waxy texture and is less abrasive. It also is more pliable in extreme cold and holds its shape better for braiding.

The best rope braiding is done internally, resulting in braids that appear to disappear into themselves. This requires some skill, however, and is not a universal practice by manufacturers and outfitters. More common is an approach employing small external loops. The problem is that these small loops may go searching for objects to snag themselves upon (obviously influenced by Murphy's Law). There is a big difference in how rope is braided, so conduct your own research before purchasing a towline.

The bungee cord should be designed to absorb shock and take up slack resulting from varying speed between you and your dog. If you both were always traveling at exactly the same speed, there would be no need for the bungee. Since this simply doesn't happen, even with experienced skijorers, the bungee is an important piece of equipment. Arctic-grade bungee is essential, because it must perform well in cold conditions. A bungee not designed for cold environments may stretch at 0 degrees Fahrenheit but not recoil to its original shape. Arctic bungee also performs well in warm weather. The best advice is to buy from knowledgeable equipment providers; there is no substitute for experience in this area. Bungee elongation and recoil properties are a function of diameter, length, temperature, etc. and will vary by manufacturer. Determining optimal configurations usually involves extensive trial and error on the part of the supplier, and a thorough knowledge of Nordic ski technique. If your supplier doesn't know V1 from V2, the chances are that your towline will perform below expectations.

The towline extends from the skijorer's belt buckle to the snap that connects to the dog's harness. The minimum length permitted under international skijoring rules is 7½ feet. Depending on sanctioning body, the maximum length is either 12 feet (ISDRA) or unlimited (IFSS). Typical lengths are 9½ feet for one dog, 11 feet for two and 12 feet for three dogs. The varying lengths are a function of speed; additional reaction time is needed with multiple dogs. In general, more dogs equates to a longer rope.

If you'll be running more than one dog, invest in a second line with a longer bungee section and longer overall rope length. Don't simply add another tugline (a short lead with snaps). It won't adequately address the added power and speed of a second or third dog.

A snap connects the towline to the dog's harness. The best snaps are made from solid Italian bronze or stainless steel. Don't compromise here. You will want snaps with maximum strength and durability in extreme conditions.

Keeping the towline high can help minimize tangles, especially when you're stopped or in the process of reversing directions (COME AROUND). Holding the towline higher than your dog will prevent

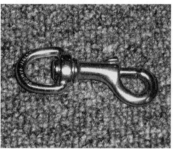

Solid bronze snap

your dog's legs from contacting the line, the main cause of tangles. The skijorer's adage "a line held high is an untangled line" is worth remembering.

Tangles can occur on the trail when the towline slackens, for example, when descending hills or skijoring over a series of small rolling hills. A slack line is also common towards the end of a run, as a dog's pace slows. New belt and towline combinations recoil a significant amount of line to address this problem, but it is still necessary for skijorers to be attentive. By keeping the line taut, or at least tight enough to keep the line away from your dog's hind legs, the chance for a tangle is significantly reduced. Skijorers can keep the line taut by reducing skiing effort, dragging their poles or snowplowing. On extended downhill sections you can also hold the line up with your hand.

Recipe for Macramé

THOR

Funny things can happen when your dogs want to run but you're talking with someone.

I'm perched at the precipice of the steepest hill at a nearby park, preparing to head downhill with my dogs in the lead. A curious cross-country skier ambles up to see what I'm up to, being unfamiliar with skijoring and not having seen a person on skis hitched up to dogs.  As I'm providing a verbal thumbnail sketch of the sport, Spot wraps around my legs, pulls me down and begins to move down the hill. Not to be outdone, Bowser unwittingly encircles the visitor and pulls her to the ground. Of course, the dogs take this as their cue to pull even more.

Together, the human and canine macramé begins a gentle slide down the hill, with the dogs' efforts to retain their balance and pull on the line only compounding the weaving action. At the bottom, after confirming that my "macramé partner" is okay, I resume my explanation of the merits of skijoring, though admittedly with diminished stature compared to a few minutes earlier.

If, or more likely *when* you experience a tangle, instruct your dog to stop (WHOA) and hold position (STAY). Then move forward so the line can drop to the ground close to your dog's feet. If the tangle is simple, i.e., one loop around one leg, there is a good chance your dog will be able to step out of the tangle. Give your dog an EASY or LINE OUT command to move him forward (slowly), but be prepared for another WHOA command if the line remains wrapped around his leg. The use of WHOA at this point will usually prevent your dog from running forward before the tangle is corrected. Unless your dog has done some serious macramé, this procedure will usually undo a tangle without the need to remove poles or gloves.

Your towline should also have reflective properties similar to those recommended for the harness and belt. Leading outfitters manufacture towlines with reflective strands interwoven throughout the length of the line. This technology makes skijorer and dog much more visible during nighttime or low-light conditions. Choose towlines made with high quality reflective "yarn" (such as 3M) for maximum reflectivity.

We've described the harness, belt and towline individually, but ideally these components function as a complete system. For example, a good system will absorb most of the shock *before* it reaches your back or your dog. The individual parts should work well together to provide optimum performance and an enjoyable outing for you and your dog.

Booties

Race car drivers know they have a lot riding on their tires, and indeed even the motorist in the lane next to you knows enough not to drive on bald or damaged tires. And so it is with your dog's feet: speed and control (and by extension, enjoyment) can only be optimized if feet, pads, nails, etc., are in good shape.

This means paying constant attention to your dog's "tires." As usual, there are a couple different levels here—first and foremost is to combine preventive measures with frequent inspections. Several examples in each category follow.

Prevention

> ▶ Know the current trail conditions.

> ▶ Have booties with you at all times.

> ▶ Avoid long runs on hard or abrasive surfaces.

> ▶ Increase distance gradually to permit your dog's foot pads to develop protective calluses.

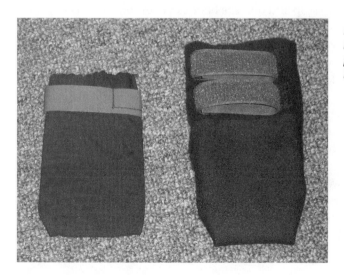

Lightweight Cordura® bootie (left); fleece/Toughtek® bootie (right)

Inspection

- ▸ Avoid excessive nail length.

- ▸ Check foot for abrasions, cuts or fissures.

- ▸ Trim hair between pads if necessary.

Avoiding potential problems requires constant vigilance. For example, that appealing gravel road that you ran with your dogs in September can be brutal on paws in December, especially without snow cover. That soft and forgiving surface may have become a slicing machine, with the gravel frozen in place and transformed into sharp and unyielding hazards.

A second level, which you will develop over time, is to watch your dog for signals. Dogs will usually communicate a wealth of information on the condition of the trail and their personal comfort, including foot condition. You simply need to know what to look for in order to tap into this near-continuous stream of information. A dog favoring one paw is trying to tell you something about that foot, while apprehensiveness may foretell poor traction or even thin ice. Even tail and ear position are indicators that can provide useful intelligence. Of course, the most obvious red flag is red snow, which means stop immediately.

Booties help protect your dog's feet from a hard, rough or abrasive surface. In such situations, it is best to have your dog wearing the booties right at the start. In other cases, you may decide once underway to stop and don the booties. An example is if the surface is soft enough but snow is beginning to build up between the pads of your dog's feet. You'll notice a "snowball" effect, and the dog will likely attempt to remove the chunks of snow at every opportunity.

Some dogs are more prone to snowballing than others, particularly those with long or fine hair that is soft to the touch. Examples include setters, collies and poodles, but you must determine your own pooch's propensity for snowballing. Putting on booties at the onset of this problem can work wonders, so you'll want to be prepared. In such conditions, make sure you clean out all the snow from between the pads before installing the bootie. An alternative to booties for the occasional dog that won't wear them is to trim the hair short between pads and apply petroleum jelly. Spray-on cooking oil can also be effective, but don't use butter flavor: your dog may find it irresistible and lick it clean.

Booties' versatility has been proven in many types of snow conditions. Perhaps even more important is that booties are key items in the first-aid kit that you should always carry for your dog. If your dog develops an abraded pad or sustains a cut from a rock or chunk of ice, you may need a bootie just to get back home. Early use of a bootie can keep your dog from aggravating the injury and from developing a negative association with skijoring. Always carry a few spare booties in case one becomes worn through, falls off and is lost, or somehow gets chewed while you've stopped on the trail to make adjustments. Booties (for use on snow) are so light that you can easily stuff a few spares into your pocket or fanny pack and not detect the extra load.

Pay close attention to snow and trail conditions when deciding whether to put booties on your dog. Snow conditions are a big factor, since freezing and thawing cycles can produce a crusty and abrasive surface. Similarly, lack of snow can turn your favorite trail into a frozen gravel paw-grinder. Frozen gravel can emulate coarse sandpaper, resulting in bleeding from toenails worn to the quick, or blown-out pads, even on short runs. Race-bred and high-energy dogs tend to experience these problems to a greater degree. This is due to working dogs' tendency to pull extremely hard when in harness. However, you should be prepared for paw problems regardless of breed, since no dog is immune and prevention is simple and effective.

Putting booties on your dog is easy, provided you let the dog do the work instead of trying to force them on a reluctant beast. A dog's natural tendency is to pull away when you attempt to put on the boot, so you'll want to anticipate this behavior and channel his energy toward achieving your goal.

Suggested Steps for Putting a Bootie on Your Dog

- ▸ Grab bootie and make sure Velcro® strap is unattached (open).

- ▸ Straddle dog so dog's head is in front of your legs. Squeeze with your knees to hold dog in place.

- ▸ Lift dog's front leg up high enough so dog can't easily pull away from bootie.

Bootie Installation

Straddle dog or place in SIT/STAY.

Clean debris from foot, including between pads (rear foot pictured).

Lift leg in natural range of motion to install bootie.

Slide bootie onto foot using fingers as guides.

Even out excess material beneath Velcro strap before securing.

Repeat previous steps for rear feet.

- Put two thumbs just inside the bootie and two index fingers on the outside of the bootie. Use your remaining fingers to keep your dog's foot in position and to guide the foot into the bootie.

- Since your dog can only move his foot downward, he will unknowingly work with you instead of against you.

- Maneuver his foot over the bottom edge of the opening of the bootie. Work the bootie up over the toenails and the rest of the foot, and pull the bootie up over the ankle.

- Secure the Velcro strap tightly. As you're doing this, evenly distribute any excess material that will tend to bunch up at the ankle. This surplus is due to the fact that the bootie is generally a constant width while the dog's ankle and foot are variable width.

- For the hind legs, reverse your stance over the dog and repeat the process. Move your dog's tail to the opposite side of the foot being booted so you can see what you're doing.

Make sure that you don't pull or extend your dog's legs beyond their normal range of motion when putting on booties. With practice you'll become a master canine cobbler.

Bootie materials include Cordura,® fleece, and Toughtek® 9000, a material used in high quality ski glove and mitten palms. Lighter boots constructed of materials such as 330-denier Cordura are easier to keep on your dog for two reasons: 1) The lighter mass makes it more difficult for a dog to kick off the bootie in full stride and 2) The thinner material allows the Velcro strap to tighten more securely and uniformly around the dog's ankle. The light weight and compact nature of these booties makes them easy to store—a dozen can fit into a small jacket pocket. Lightweight booties are usually the least expensive choice and perform exceptionally well in most situations. However, they tend to wear out quickly when used off snow and are not suitable for very abrasive conditions such as frozen gravel.

Heavier booties are preferred in abrasive or icy conditions. They are usually made of heavyweight Cordura or a combination of fleece and Toughtek 9000, which performs well in icy conditions. Because of the extra weight and thickness, it is best to purchase them with two Velcro straps on each bootie rather than one.

Bootie Checklist

TRAIL TYPE/CONDITION	BOOTIES NEEDED?		NOTES
	For pet or average puller	For race dog or hard puller	
Groomed snow	NO	NO	Booties are not necessary for most dogs on groomed trails.
Ungroomed snow	NO	NO	Breaking trail in fresh snow does not require booties unless dog is susceptible to snowballing.
Snow with ice glaze on surface	YES	YES	This type of snow will abrade the top of the toenail area when the dog's foot punches through the glaze.
Crunchy, crusty or abrasive snow	YES	YES	Test with bare hands. Push against snow with body weight.
Snow temperature and moisture content conducive to snowball formation	YES (if prone to snowballing)	NO	Race dogs rarely have snowballing problems, perhaps due to breed and foot action during gait.
Packed dirt	NO	NO	Dirt trails rarely require booties, though surface becomes hard when frozen, limiting shock absorption. Avoid long runs on frozen dirt with any dog to minimize impact stress.
Grass	NO	NO	This is the most forgiving trail type for working dogs.
Sand	NO	NO	Frozen sand trails can require booties for race dogs on long runs.
Gravel road	Possibly	Possibly	Size, type of stone and amount of sand on road determines need for booties. Check pads for wear after short distance. Frozen gravel roads require booties unless distance is very short.
Cement or asphalt	Probably not	YES	Race dogs will wear down pads and toenails very quickly on this type of trail, especially for fresh dogs held under 15 mph. Avoid long runs on cement or asphalt with any dog to minimize impact stress.

Checklist continued on next page

Bootie Checklist, continued			
TRAIL TYPE/CONDITION	**BOOTIES NEEDED?**		**NOTES**
	For pet or average puller	*For race dog or hard puller*	
Wood chip trails	NO	NO	Wood chips usually don't require booties and are excellent for shock absorption. Check feet often on trail since wood chips vary in size and shape and can lodge between pads. Race dogs on long runs may need booties to protect foot webbing.
Crushed gravel	Possibly	Possibly	Crushed gravel trails vary widely. Use booties if stones are sharp or run is long.
General notes for all trails	Allow your dog's feet time to adapt to any type of trail. Like a human hand or foot, it takes time for a pad to toughen and form protective calluses.		
	Use booties whenever pads show signs of wear or when toenails are near the quick, regardless of trail type.		
	Your dog's feet are 100% your responsibility. A blown-out pad can take over two weeks to heal. Always carry booties when running your dog!		
	Many factors affect the need for booties on trails without snow, including abrasiveness, speed, traction and pulling force. For example, a fresh dog held to 12 mph on a frozen gravel road can wear down pads and nails in less than a mile. The same dog could run several miles at 17 mph on the same road at the end of a run and experience minimal wear.		

This extra strap increases the likelihood that the booties will stay on your dog's feet. If your dog still kicks off her booties, try securing them with duct tape. One wrap around each leg is adequate. Before using duct tape, you should try a small amount in a test area on your dog, to ensure that the tape isn't removing large amounts of fur.

Always remove booties immediately when you've completed your outing. You already know that dogs love to chew, and that they will eventually chew anything attached to their body that is within reach. Removing and storing the booties properly ensures that they'll be dry and ready to go on your next trip. Also, because booties must be tightly attached to keep them from falling off, there is a risk that they will impair circulation if left on for extended periods. If your dog tries to walk on a foot that has fallen asleep, he may trip or sprain the foot. So it's best to eliminate this risk entirely by removing booties when no longer needed.

With a little creativity, you can get many miles out of your dog's booties. First, keep your dog's toenails trimmed short to reduce their tendency to prematurely wear through the bootie material. With even moderate use, your dog will eventually wear through the bottom of the bootie. If you discover a hole before it becomes too large, you can simply flip the bootie over and use the other side. Be sure to clean any debris out of the bootie by turning it upside down while whisking your finger back and forth inside. Remember that the bootie now has a hole in it, so snow and debris can easily work their way in. Rear booties tend to wear out first, since there is more force on a dog's rear feet.

MURPHY'S LAW: BOOTIES

Skijorers will quickly note that booties tend to cluster in odd-numbered groups as opposed to pairs. For example, when in need of booties on the trail, you will be able to rapidly locate a single bootie if two are desired or three booties if a set of four is required. Researchers have been attempting to link this phenomenon with the well-known behavior of fugitive socks and mittens, and some have even speculated that wayward booties may ultimately arrive at the same location as lost socks and mittens. (See Jacque Tomlinson's *Lost Skijoring Booties: Corroboration of Black Hole Theory or Validation of Murphy's Law?* HaakNot Press.)

One observed exception to this principle occurs when skijoring with dogs having an odd number of legs. Though not a common occurrence, in some cases dedicated canines that have lost a limb to illness or injury are still on the skijoring trail, pulling with their big hearts and enjoying the experience. In this situation, booties will of course tend to congregate in even-numbered groups.

Clothing

A simple rule regarding clothing is to use the layering approach followed by many outdoor enthusiasts: use two or three thin, removable layers of clothing instead of one bulky layer. As outdoor temperatures and your body's heat output vary, you can remove or add layers to compensate. Besides improving your comfort, this approach also minimizes perspiration buildup if the first layer is a wicking material such as polypropylene. You'll appreciate this aspect later in the day when temperatures cool down and you're still dry.

Besides being "modular," clothing should be snug, yet flexible. Overly loose clothing permits air gaps, which reduce warmth and may also increase chafing. The skijoring belt should be positioned over your primary or secondary layer, but not over the outside layer. Putting the belt over the outside layer can inhibit your skiing movement, especially if the outside layer is of a nonstretch material (such as a nylon windbreaker). The best strategy is to drape your final layer over your skijor belt.

In wilderness areas, bright clothing is recommended. This is especially true if hunting is permitted in or near the area where you will be skijoring.

Eyewear

Protective eyewear is sometimes overlooked but is always important. It is a must for skijorers or bikejorers, because dogs frequently kick up snow or ice in the winter and gravel or dirt in other seasons. Glasses should be made of impact-resistant polycarbonate material or at least be designed to minimize hazards upon breakage. Other considerations are UV/ultraviolet protection and peripheral screening. These aspects increase in importance in snow-oriented sports, when excessive or prolonged reflection off the snow can cause headache and mental fatigue.

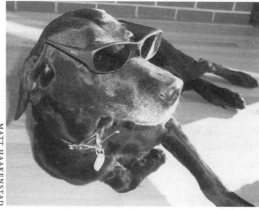

MATT HAAKENSTAD

Good eyewear is important and fashionable.

The Neckline

You can skip this section if you will be skijoring with a single dog, since a neckline is used to join two dogs. You may want to skim this information in case you decide to try pairing your dog with another while out on the trail.

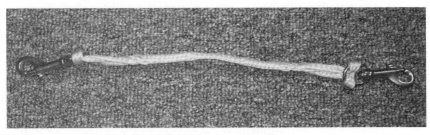

Necklines are generally 14" long and connect two dogs at the collar.

A neckline connects two lead dogs and encourages them to function as a cohesive unit. A neckline can help prevent your dogs from turning in opposite directions, from stopping at scent posts or from pursuing small game. One dog that is a good leader can help encourage a second dog to follow your commands. However, a neckline will be of no help if both dogs decide to chase a squirrel!

The neckline attaches to the metal ring in each collar. The collars should be quite snug; otherwise, one dog may pull the collar off of the other, resulting in an empty collar being dragged down the trail. Start by fitting two fingers underneath the collar. This fit ensures adequate tightness without discomfort for the dog.

The best collars are of the same material and width (one inch) as the dog harness. Leather is not a good choice due to its tendency to stretch when wet. Avoid plastic connectors and instead select metal hardware for strength and durability.

When running two dogs at lead it is a good idea to periodically switch the dogs back and forth, i.e., from right to left and vice versa. This will familiarize your dogs with either side when running as coleaders. This ambidextrous quality becomes important when a tangle requires your dogs to switch positions. Otherwise, dogs tend to favor one side over the other and may resist switching when you need them to do so. They may even try to jump over the other dog to get to a favored side.

A neckline is a versatile piece of equipment that can be used for improvising when necessary. Consider carrying one when skijoring, or keep a spare in the glove box of your car. A neckline can be used to repair a line, replace a malfunctioning snap, or as a short lead to connect to a dog.

If your dog is involved in a major tangle, first disconnect the neckline. This removes one of the connection points and makes it easier to undo the rest of the macramé. Remember that the neckline is always an easy line to find since it is attached to your dog's head. Finally, make sure you reconnect the neckline before resuming skijoring.

Belt Attachment/Accessory Pouch

This piece of equipment is optional, but once you've tried one, you'll probably never leave home without it. A fanny pack kit is designed to attach to your skijor belt. It is secured by Velcro straps and can be removed if you're just out for a quick lap or want to lighten your load for a race. Look for a fanny pack that has a reflective strip on the back, for those occasions when you're out after dark.

The fanny pack makes a sturdy and secure carrier when centered on the back of your skijor belt. The inside pouch works well for carrying ski wax, booties, water, etc., and can also accommodate the light windbreaker you've removed after warming up. Some fanny packs have outside mesh pouches that are handy for carrying away "used dog food" deposited by your dog along the trail.

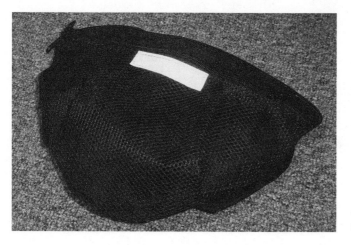

Fanny pack with mesh outer pocket

The following testimonial illustrates the importance of using good equipment, fitting and attaching it properly, and carrying redundant accessories. Having a dog that comes when called doesn't hurt either.

Turbocharged

HELGA

Helga had recently been introduced to the sport of skijoring and was eager to learn. She had borrowed a dog named Turbo from a friend so she could sample the sport. Turbo was an Alaskan husky with race experience, for which her friend had paid around $500. Turbo was young and energetic and had demonstrated a willingness to pull and run hard. Helga could hardly wait to hit the trail and see what Turbo could do. Things started out well and in no time they were flying down the trail.

Helga didn't notice that the towline borrowed from her friend was badly frayed. Turbo roared ahead, pulling even better than Helga had expected, and she skied hard to do her share. While the two established a rhythm, the towline marched to its own beat. A strand popping here, a thread snapping there, and soon precious few fibers remained intact. Suddenly, as they rounded a bend and headed into the woods, the towline broke!

Turbo went blasting ahead, delighted with the opportunity to accelerate on the approach into the forest. The loss of tension in the towline sent Helga sprawling backward in an ungraceful landing in the fluffy snow. She sat up and spied Turbo rounding the turn before entering the woods. "Turbo" she sang out, hoping he might be favorably disposed to respond. He seemed to run a little faster, and she envisioned a crisp $500 bill with wings, flying upward into the clouds. Why, that appeared to be Turbo's face on the $500 bill! "Turrr-Bo!!!" she screamed as she jumped to her feet, determined to interrupt his trek into the woods and onto a trail network that extended for over 100 km. Something in her voice caused Turbo to tilt his head and look back, still without breaking stride. To Helga's surprise, when the energetic husky saw her, he immediately made a U-turn and headed back to where she stood.

"GOOD DOG" she declared as he approached, not completely believing her luck. As their eyes met, she discerned a decidedly nonplussed look which seemed to ask, "What are you doing standing back here?" "GOOD DOG," she reaffirmed as she took a neckline from her pocket to repair the broken towline. The duo resumed their journey into the forest, at least one of them now a bit wiser about the merits of using good equipment and being prepared.

Skis and Bindings, Poles, Boots, Ski Wax

Standard cross-country ski gear is used in skijoring. Ski equipment is obviously very important and is listed last in this section only because the focus is on equipment unique to skijoring. In addition, many potential skijorers already own cross-country ski equipment. Either skate-skiing or classic-style equipment can be used, as described in Chapter Three. Ski poles are used in skijoring, though poles are often omitted by beginners until they are comfortable skiing behind their dog.

If you already own ski equipment, there is no need to replace or upgrade it in order to try the sport. Avoid metal-edged skis; they are unnecessary on the ski trail and may pose a danger to your dog. If you don't own skis, poles or boots, it's a good idea to borrow or rent first to help define your preferences before purchasing. And if you use waxable classic skis, remember to bring the correct wax.

MURPHY'S LAW: WAX FOR CROSS-COUNTRY SKIS

The correct wax for current temperature and snow conditions is generally available; however, it was the one deemed least likely to be needed and was left in the car.

Corollary 1

Any attempt to retrieve this wax from your automobile, once skijoring is underway, will cause disequilibrium in the weather gradient. Put another way, retrieving the correct wax will cause weather conditions to change so that the retrieved wax is no longer the correct wax.

Corollary 2

The need to wax is inversely proportional to the time available to apply the wax. The greater the need, the less time available.

Corollary 3

Harder, cold-weather waxes should always be applied first, allowing softer, warmer-weather waxes to be applied easily on top of harder waxes. Therefore, one will always gravitate toward applying waxes that are too soft and are for warmer conditions than those actually present. The soft wax must then be scraped off to allow the correct wax to be applied (see Corollary 4).

Corollary 4
The piece of equipment inadvertently omitted from the wax kit (other than the correct wax) is most likely to be the scraper, used for removing old wax.

Corollary 5
If only one wax is available, either in your wax kit or at a retail counter located in time of desperate need, it will always be klister.

This chapter has described the equipment used in skijoring. Chapter 9 details the equipment necessary for warm weather alternatives to skijoring, including canicross, bikejoring and rollerjoring. Although some pieces of equipment are interchangeable, we recommend reading Chapter 9 before running, biking or skating behind your dog.

CHAPTER SEVEN

The Stewardship

Once you reach a point where skijoring is a combination of fun, excitement, challenge and passion, you will be ready to help promote and preserve the sport. For some persons this happens after they've become comfortable with the rudimentary aspects of control and realize they're hooked. For others it happens on the first time out. In any case, at some point the skijorer may be drawn to help ensure the continued acceptance of the sport and the availability of trails that will accommodate dogs.

This realization may initially be nothing more than the desire to clean up after, properly train and control your dog. If you'd like to learn more, some areas have associations or clubs devoted to skijoring or dog sledding. These groups are usually very receptive and can be a great resource for newcomers to dog-powered sports. If you have such an organization in your vicinity, you may want to attend one of their meetings. Check with a ski or outdoor store about skijoring or dog sledding clubs in your area. You can also try searching on the Internet under keywords such as "skijor" or "skijoring," "dog sledding," "dog mushing," etc.

Multi-use trail

Over time the realization may expand to include additional effort—perhaps getting more involved in a club, working to acquire and maintain more local skijor trails, or helping to educate others. If you're unable to locate a skijor club in your area, consider starting one. Tips for starting a club are included later in this chapter. You'll be rewarded for your efforts with an expanding set of friends who love dogs and the outdoors, with an increased knowledge of the sport, and with a new awareness of trail networks and the people that make them possible.

Trail Access
THOR

As with many things in life, it's easy to take trail access for granted. If we all just do the small things, like cleaning up after our party, skijoring will be well-received by other trail users. Not all trail users adore (or even care for) dogs, so we need to go out of our way to make everyone feel welcome and comfortable on the trail.

The key is being prepared before hitting the trail. This means giving your dog the opportunity to do his business BEFORE starting out, as well as bringing along several plastic bags for any "projects" that are completed during the actual trail run.

> *Trail Access*
> ## SPOT

I'm an ardent supporter of multi-use trails. There are usually much better smells along a trail that is used by not only people, but also dogs, horses, rabbits, and so forth. I do wish that there were more cats on the trail, however, as this would open up a new dimension to the sport.

Humans are definitely an intriguing species. Why is it that they delight in picking up and packaging the solid waste that I leave along the trail? I've observed that many owners have a penchant for collecting things, but this one seems a bit dysfunctional. It deprives other dogs of the opportunity to stop and check out my work.

Basic Level—Cleaning Up after You and Your Dog

Try to leave the trail in a condition at least as good as it was when you found it. Don't hesitate to pick up any small items of trash left by other skiers. If even half of us did this, essentially all trails would be pristine. It's probably a stretch to expect anyone to interrupt their stride (or their dog's) to stop and pick up excrement left by someone else's animal. However, please consider doing this if it was left in an offensive location, or at least kick it off the trail into the woods. Remember, we're all ambassadors for just about everything we're engaged in, and perhaps even more so for activities like skijoring that are not widely known or understood.

MATT HAAKENSTAD

At a minimum, you must always clean up any solid waste deposited by your dog. If you're unable to do this during your skijor run, return to the trail after you've watered and secured your dog in your vehicle.

If possible, get your dog to do her business at home before you start down the trail. Dogs are more likely to do their business at home, where they are more comfortable and there are fewer distractions. While not always possible, this is

---

well worth a try, since success greatly reduces the chances that you'll need to deal with this issue on the trail. Try getting your dog to "drop" before hitting the trail by letting her run free in the backyard or by playing catch or your favorite chasing game with her.

Once underway, your dog will usually telegraph to you an impending need to relieve herself. This is your signal to immediately move the dog off the trail, whether the issue is solid or liquid waste.

Dogs are wonderfully efficient machines, able to muster tremendous running and pulling power. Ever the ecologically smart creation, they do this without producing any airborne pollutants or harmful byproducts. However, Murphy would point out that one doesn't get something for nothing. Dogs do produce some waste products, sometimes employing . . .

The Poop Spreader
SPOT

Here we go, blasting down the trail. Feels good to get off the couch. But I wish Ol' Two Legs had given me a chance to sniff & strut for a few minutes prior to hitting the trail. Thought he knew we both benefit if he lets me lighten my load before we take off. Otherwise, nature will probably call once I start running hard. The skeptics in the crowd should try getting down on all fours and running hard (the way it's supposed to be done, by the way) while in harness. If I'm gonna put out, I need to first clear out. It's that simple. I mean, if you were going to race one of those contraptions that some dogs love to chase (I believe humans refer to them as "cars"), would you want it loaded with excess baggage? Didn't think so. It's no different with your favorite canine athlete.

So there we are booking along, and I need to go NOW. Here goes - I'll try to make it quick. What's this? Thor doesn't slow down for me, skies right past and actually pulls me along for a couple of dog lengths. How totally rude! Well, at least he doesn't run into me. I shoot him a peeved glance, which finally brings him around, but not before I've covered a pretty wide area. Not a big deal, except this makes more work for other dogs coming along later—more sniffing to figure out who was here, what I had for breakfast, my view on individual property rights and territorial issues, and so on.

Remember, your goal is to leave no trace on the trail. This is much easier if your dog does his business off to the side of the trail. Excrement in the center of the trail can be extremely offensive

This antic seems to happen just as you're hitting your stride. Suddenly and without warning, your canine friend halts mid-trail and begins to defecate. No problem so far; this is a natural thing for dogs to do. The problem arises when the skijorer has momentum or is descending a hill, making a quick stop unlikely. I recall this happening once while skijoring with Spot. I ended up passing him by and pulled him along for several feet, causing him to distribute his "work" along the ski trail. His look was most ungrateful, as if to say "Fine, so you're apparently on a schedule, but please realize I'm not moving until I complete this project." I then scrambled to clean up before the skijor team right behind us came around the bend. "Brown klister" is not welcome on trails. It's a ski stopper!

Skijor racers will typically plan their prerace preparation so their dogs have adequate time to relieve themselves prior to a training run or race. While not always an easy thing to coordinate, it is always well worth pursuing to minimize the odds of you having to stop and do the cleanup routine on the middle of the trail.

---

to cross-country skiers. Consider that some elite skiers may have nearly $50 worth of fluorocarbon wax on their skis and will not be happy about smearing their ski surface with waste from your dog. These same people will immediately recall even a single incident at the time you are requesting access for skijoring on cross-country trails in your area.

Always carry several plastic bags with you for picking up solid waste. Inspect these bags for holes before starting out, for obvious reasons. One approach is the double bag system, in which you turn one bag inside-out and use it like a glove to grab the waste. Peel the "glove" back off your hand so that the waste is now contained inside the bag, and seal the bag with as little trapped air as possible (force the air out downwind, and don't inhale!). Food storage bags work well for this task, as do the plastic bags sometimes provided with your home-delivered daily newspaper (heavier plastic is better). Turning the bag inside out before picking up the waste is especially important when using a sealing plastic bag.

Next, enclose this bag in a second bag, force out as much air as possible, then seal and stow in a fanny pack or pocket. Some trails

---

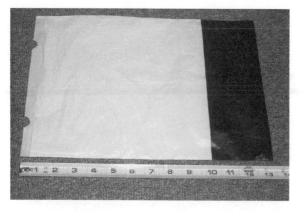

Double-ply bag for pet waste

have waste receptacles along the way, unless of course you'd like to take your souvenir home with you. If your dog did his business on the trail, kick a small amount of clean snow over the affected area before resuming your skijor run.

Many pet supply stores sell excellent bags made specifically for picking up dog waste. Sold in boxes, these double bags are just like the ones provided at some trails and are much easier to use than single plastic bags.

MURPHY'S LAW: DOG WASTE CARRYING BAG

Basic tenet

Your need for a poop bag is a function of whether or not you remembered to bring the bag. If you've forgotten to bring the bag, you will most certainly need it. On the other hand, bringing the bag greatly increases the probability that you will not need it. (The mathematics that describe this probability function are beyond the scope of this text, and the reader is referred to the fine work by Conrad Carnauba [*Mathematical Modeling of the Relationship between Visiting the Carwash and the Meteorological Propensity for Rain: A Treatise,* HaakNot Press] for a lucid discussion of an analogous and equally vexing problem. One may use the same equations developed by Carnauba in the skijoring case, but be careful to modify the coefficients, or you may inadvertently cause rain by forgetting your poop bag.)

Corollary 1

If "x" is the number of poop bags that you will actually need on your skijoring outing, the number you'll remember to bring along is always "x minus 1."

Corollary 2

The probability of your dog having to poop in the middle of the trail is directly proportional to the number of observers in the immediate vicinity. A large gathering of spectators virtually assures that your dog will stop and do her business in a location that is visible to the maximum number of persons.

Corollary 3

The volume of waste produced by your dog is also directly proportional to the size of the audience, not the size of the dog. In front of a crowd, there is no reliable relationship between the size of the dog and volume of waste produced.

Corollary 4

Dog owners will display exaggerated visual antics when cleaning up after their dog, especially when other persons are in the vicinity. Melodramatic flaunting of plastic bags is typical, as the owner attempts to convey in no uncertain terms that he or she is not one of the DDDMs (Deadbeat Dog Dads or Moms) responsible for abandoned dog waste encountered on the trail.

Dog Control

Dog owners have a special responsibility as custodian of their skijoring "locomotive." There are several different dimensions to this, depending on whether they are interacting with pedestrians, cross-country skiers or other skijoring parties.

Persons who don't own dogs or are not familiar with them may

Sometimes loose or stray dogs will run alongside when you come by with your dog or team. They may run along with your dogs for perhaps 50 to 100 yards or more, attracted by the sight, sounds and commotion. In most cases the loose dog will drop back fairly quickly, especially if you can keep your dog or dogs focused on the trail and on moving forward.

But this does highlight two key issues. First, the more that your dog responds to your ON BY command and continues pulling forward, the better. The best case scenario is to get him to virtually ignore the loose dog and put his energy into the task at hand. Second, skijorers and dog owners should not permit their dogs to run loose anywhere near an active trail. Dog owners must have control of their pets at all times and not allow them to become a distraction, an irritant or even a danger to other dogs and humans.

It is best to avoid contact with loose dogs in the first place. If you see a dog roaming on the trail, steer your team away from the potential distraction. You may also consider stopping your team and alerting the dog's owner, if nearby. If contact is made with a loose dog, continue moving your team down the trail and leave the area.

be intrigued or intimidated by your canine, or may have some other unexpected reaction. The point is that you cannot predict or control the person's behavior; therefore you must be in control of your dog. If you are at all unsure of how your dog may react to an approaching stranger or dog, you must avoid any potential contact. In other words, if there is any chance that your dog may act aggressively, *don't provide the opportunity for this to occur.* Never was the adage "An ounce of prevention is worth a pound of cure" more relevant.

Maintain a good rapport with other Nordic skiers or pedestrians by being proactive. Do whatever it takes to make fellow trail users feel comfortable and not inconvenienced or threatened. Even if you are "legally permitted" on a specific trail, view yourself as a guest and behave accordingly. Keep your dog close and work hard to avoid tangles with other trail users. Warn others on approach and tell your dog ON BY.

If you do stop to talk, remember that your dog is a master of the tangle. Move your dog off to the side of the trail so that you don't block others from skiing through. If you encounter other trail users who are upset for some reason, stay confident and calm. It may help to remind yourself of your goal of leaving a favorable impression on whomever you encounter. Perhaps someday North American trails will resemble those in Scandinavia, where dogs are widely accepted.

Passing Other Trail Users

Be careful when overtaking skiers who are not skijoring. Let them know you're coming up to avoid startling them. One suggestion is to have your dog slow down as you approach by snowplowing and using the EASY command. Feel free to shout "Hello" and "Thank you" as you go by. Indicate which side you'll be passing on—for example, "on your left." Be careful not to accidentally hit the "passee" with your poles on the way by. And always be sure that you are skiing in the correct direction of travel. Following these simple suggestions will help ensure that other skiers will be happy to have both you and your dog on the trail.

Other skijorers traveling with their dogs present a different set of challenges. Here the main concern is appropriate interaction between their dog and your own. This becomes much easier with experience, but initially you must make sure you understand how your own dog will react. Again, since you cannot control the behavior of the other dog you must control that of your own. Choke up on the towline if necessary for added control. There is zero tolerance for aggressive canine behavior in skijoring. The best approach is to train your dog to respond appropriately before exposing him to a public situation. If your dog acts aggressively toward another dog, you must correct the behavior immediately. A dog that persists in this type of behavior should be sternly disciplined in a private setting, using established obedience training techniques.

Skijorers being passed should slow their team so that ample distance is maintained between parties (more detail is provided in Chapter 8, "The Racing Experience"). Avoid back-and-forth passing games when skijoring.

Use special caution wherever dogs and their owners are mingling in groups, such as before a race or at a fun run. Many people don't

The local bike path can become a skijoring trail in winter.

manage this situation particularly well and have a tendency to socialize with other skijorers while ignoring their dogs. This often results in tangles and an increased chance for aggressive behavior. Of course, tangled dogs tend to blame each other for the tangle. Regaining control of the situation can be difficult when one is on skis in close quarters. Never position yourself between quarreling dogs—instead, pull them apart by using the towline or harness as you shout NO! An even better option is to avoid such adventures entirely by keeping your dog completely separated from other dogs, unless both owners understand how their dog reacts to other dogs and agree in advance to their interaction.

And mentioned previously but worth repeating: Assume that anything your dog does wrong is your fault. This tenet increases the likelihood that the owner will stay cool during a mishap and puts the emphasis on the owner being a good teacher.

Promoting the Sport: Trail Access

One of the challenges facing the sport of skijoring concerns venues: Where can skijorers go to enjoy their sport? Many communities have a trail network for summer activities such as walking, hiking,

Keep Out Means You!

HELGA

The dogs are energized on our bikejoring run in the brisk autumn air. The towline is tight as I soak up the fall colors surrounding the seldom used gravel road. In the distance, a large municipal city services dump truck about a half  mile away is coming in our direction. The vehicle is so large that it completely hoards the trail; if the trail is about 8 feet across, the truck is at least 10 feet wide. The dense shrub and tree growth surrounding the trail make it completely impossible to bikejor around the obstacle. I don't want to confront this beast and be forced to stand off in the trees with Bowser and Spot while it groans and lumbers past. Instead, I make a command decision to take a smaller side trail that cuts off and heads up into a heavily forested area. This trail loops up and around for about two miles before returning to the gravel road. My plan is to simply run the loop and return to the main trail after the vehicle has passed.

Unfortunately, that fork leads up into a section of the trail that is clearly posted as off-limits to the public. There are signs everywhere. Apparently there is some logging occurring in this section and they don't want people in that area. After bikejoring around this verboten loop, I prepare to return to the main trail; but am dismayed to encounter the smoldering behemoth truck coming right up the same trail!

I literally have nowhere to go, both cornered and caught red-handed. To make things worse, as we stand alongside the trail, my dogs immediately wrap the towline around several small trees and my bike, creating world-class macramé. Not only am I a "violator," but I can't even move. I know I'm about to be the recipient of a lecture and tongue lashing from the driver of the approaching vehicle.

My expectation is fulfilled, and the city employee is relentless in his admonishment of the wayward bikejorer. The driver seizes his opportunity to be king for a moment, enjoying this variation from the normal routine of picking up sewer drains. Eventually the worker runs out of things to say, as my strategy of listening, apologizing and amicably nodding pays off. He turns me loose, with a final warning not to use the trail again. The dogs seem even more overjoyed than normal when I finally say LET'S GO and we quickly leave the city truck behind.

biking, inline skating, etc., which double as cross-country ski trails (and in some cases, snowshoe or snowmobile trails) in the winter. The multiseasonal use aspect of many trails helps justify their existence and maintenance by local government, private parties or volunteer organizations.

The challenge emerges when dogs are added to the equation— not unlike the problem created when horses are allowed on trails. True, dogs are much smaller than horses, but their inclusion can affect trail dynamics. Skijoring is typically permitted on multi-use trails, though skijorers should always confirm this prior to showing up with their dogs. If you're unable to confirm or are otherwise unsure about the acceptability of skijoring on a particular trail, use the trail during off-peak times such as early morning or late evening. Wear a headlamp if necessary.

One way to increase access is to ensure that enough multi-use trails are available, both through maintaining existing trails and by working to acquire additional trails. Recreational trail use in urban areas is up sharply in recent years, which has both a negative and a positive effect. The negative is that more people are attempting to share the limited resource of trail space, and this can lead to confrontation and debate. Also, many suburban developers have their sights set on unprotected trails, since they're usually located on prime real estate that would earn them a significant financial return. However, the positive effect is that with more people interested in trails as a natural resource, it becomes easier to defend and enhance existing trails and to secure additional trails.

This is an area where skijorers can have a significant impact. By educating other skijorers on proper and courteous use of skijoring trails and by enlightening the public on the fascinating aspects of skijoring, it becomes possible to participate in the effort to obtain and preserve adequate trail resources.

If you'd like to expand trail access, a good place to start is at a local outdoor sports store that sells skiing or camping equipment. These stores have a vested interest in promoting the sport (remember, skijoring also requires skis, bindings, poles, boots, wax and so on). Many stores will hold seminars on equipment and technique and can assist with efforts to increase and retain trail access. Also check with your local park system on trail access, regulations, conditions and plans for future development.

Adding to the network of trails available for skijoring is always a

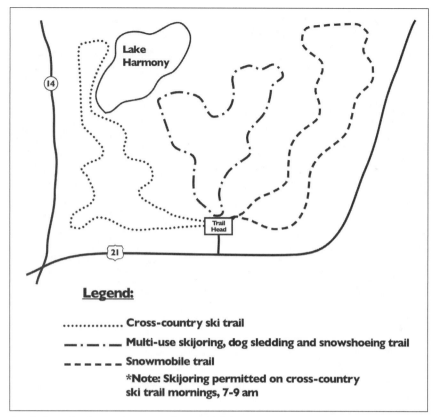

Legend:

.... Cross-country ski trail

—.—.— Multi-use skijoring, dog sledding and snowshoeing trail

— — — — Snowmobile trail

*Note: Skijoring permitted on cross-country ski trail mornings, 7-9 am

A well-planned trail network accommodates multiple interests.

worthwhile cause. Besides providing more variety, it also decreases dog density and thus relieves pressure on existing trails. Obtaining the exclusive use of a trail for skijoring from a local park or refuge is an ambitious but possibly unrealistic goal (at least until skijoring becomes popular in your community). Many park systems are short of resources and are not likely to fund a dedicated skijoring trail until justified by demand.

Instead, try to obtain access to multi-use trails that would be shared with skiers, snowshoers, mushers, horses, etc. Cross-country skiers will probably prefer ski-only trails, while horses usually aren't that prevalent in the winter months. The result may well be a great, accessible trail for skijoring without the need for justification on an exclusive basis. Note that some multi-use trails require increased vigilance: equestrian trails, for example, may have deep holes that

Outdoor trade shows can be a good source for skijoring information.

are dangerous to your dog. Ski horse trails first by yourself to confirm that the route is safe for your dog.

Another access solution is the time-share approach. This method permits skijorers access to the trail or section of trail during specified times only. For example, one lit Nordic ski trail in Minnesota designates one to two hours for skijoring one night a week. When trail conditions are good, a dog running on a trail produces an impact comparable to that of ski poles. And of course you'll stress that skijorers are conscientious about cleaning up after their dogs (and then work to ensure that skijorers comply with this requirement).

Park managers are proponents of outdoor recreation and take pride in developing and maintaining their trail networks. They strive to appeal to a diverse group of individuals, including families, winter sport enthusiasts, pet owners, etc. They are also interested in promoting new uses for their trails, especially as an activity grows in popularity. Snowshoeing is a good example.

By emphasizing the benefits of skijoring for human and dog, and that skijoring does not negatively impact trails or other trail users, you increase the chances that park management will support skijoring. Usually this support will take the form of a trial involving a restricted and monitored trail. Typically the experiment

STARTING A SKIJORING CLUB

The following tips may be helpful if you decide to start a skijoring club in your area:

▸ Team up with one or two other skijorers to share insights and develop a plan.

▸ Contact a local mushing club for ideas. A mushing club is an excellent source for information on mushing and skijoring. Mushing and skijoring clubs share a common interest in promoting and educating the public about dog-powered sports.

▸ Ask for permission to display a skijoring flyer at skiing or outdoor-oriented stores in your area. The announcement should contain a skijoring photograph and a basic description of the sport and should say "new club forming" or similar wording.

▸ Develop an e-mail list to disseminate information, coordinate meetings, and schedule clinics and fun runs. An e-mail list is also effective for answering beginners' questions or for seasoned skijorers to share their perspectives.

▸ Request a display booth at an outdoor trade show. Have dogs, equipment, pictures and skijoring information available, along with one or more skijorers to explain the sport and answer questions from attendees. This is a great opportunity to provide information about events planned for your club.

will be evaluated after the season to assess usage and reaction from other trail users.

During a trial season, be proactive and touch base with other groups to ensure the acceptance of skijoring. Be prepared to tactfully and diplomatically answer questions concerning trail impact. Typical questions might include waste left on the trail, dog foot depressions and potential for accidents between skijorers and other trail users. A thank-you note sent to the trail owner, manager, park district or groomer is a nice gesture that can help build rapport.

General notes on trail courtesy include keeping your dog from running in the classic tracks on those trails that are groomed for both skate skiing and classic cross-country skiing. You should also refrain from taking a sick dog to a skijoring area and keep your dog's vaccinations current. Don't skijor on very soft snow unless

K.H. RAUBUCH

the trail is already in a deteriorated state. Be prepared for curious onlookers asking questions after you finish.

One of the best ways to promote skijoring is also the most fun—simply get out and do it! Possibly the best advertisement for the sport is a person with his or her dog, out having fun, with the dog clearly enjoying himself as well. This is a perfect occasion to demonstrate responsible behavior, including dog handling and cleanup. If you're on a trail where few skijorers have traveled, you will probably turn a few heads.

Being a good steward of skijoring can be a rewarding way to give something back to the sport. You can control your level of involvement, from simply being a responsible participant to assisting with some of the other opportunities described above. And best of all, you're encouraged to get out and set a good example, on the trail!

CHAPTER EIGHT

The Racing Experience

K.H. RAUBUCH

Racing Primer

Skijor racing can be an excellent way to develop and hone many of the skills that we've discussed. The very nature of racing forces you to pay attention to your dog, to your own body, and to the many variables that influence the sport. Racing is also a great opportunity to observe other skijorers and their dogs—including those in both the "how to" and "how *not* to" categories. These factors can all help to greatly shorten your learning curve for the sport.

Racing is about having fun, and it helps to keep this perspective if you decide to participate. Of course being competitive adds to the enjoyment, but go easy on yourself (and your dog) and accept that you probably won't be competitive in your first several races. Your primary objective should be to enjoy the experience and absorb as much new knowledge as possible.

Your first race will be more successful if you're prepared, have an understanding of racing rules and know what to expect on the course. Reviewing this chapter will give you a feel for the basic rules and flavor of racing. If you focus on having fun in your first race, and don't set your expectations too high, you might just be pleasantly surprised.

Racing Requirements and Prerace Preparation

Skijorers of all ability levels and experience, including first-time racers, are welcome at skijor races.

Entrants' abilities determine the class in which they compete. Beginners are encouraged to start out in the Sport, or Recreational, class. In some races, officials will decide whether skiers are eligible to compete in the Pro, or Advanced, class. The Pro class is usually populated with seasoned skijorers and has more stringent requirements for racers and their dogs. Top finishers in the Pro class usually win cash prizes.

Race classes may be combined at the discretion of race officials. Classes are usually mixed-gender, except at World Cup races, where men and women race in separate categories.

Sport classes are commonly divided into One- and Two-Dog categories; Pro classes may be divided into One-, Two- and Three-Dog categories. Don't be surprised if there's only one category for all skijorers at your first race. Skijoring is a growing sport and it's common for races to have fewer than 20 participants.

In races spanning multiple days, there is normally a requirement that the same dogs be used each day. Dogs are usually marked with paint to help enforce this rule. However, fewer dogs can be raced on second and subsequent days if a dog becomes ill or is not contributing. For safety reasons, race officials may limit the number of dogs that participants are allowed to use.

There is usually no need to purchase special equipment for racing, because most of the items are part of the standard skijoring package. Races generally require that all equipment be in good working order and safe for skijorer and dog. Chapter 6 contains detailed descriptions and photographs of recommended skijoring equipment.

Nordic skating or classic skis are permitted at skijoring races. Metal edge skis are prohibited due to the potential for injury.

A skijor belt is required equipment for racing; tow bars (similar to handles used in water skiing) are not allowed. The belt should be padded and at least three inches wide. It must also have a quick-release mechanism that remains attached to the belt and does not follow the loose line down the trail upon release. The quick-release must be positioned within arm's reach of the skijorer and must release under load. Carabiners, bolt snaps and similar locking devices are not considered acceptable quick-release mechanisms.

Towlines are generally required to have an internal bungee (inside the rope rather than outside) for safety reasons. A minimum of 15 inches of Arctic grade bungee inside the towline is recommended for shock absorption and line recoil. There are also minimum and maximum lengths for the distance between skijorer and dog (usually defined by towline length). Typical minimum length allowed is 8 feet with a maximum of 12 feet, although IFSS international rules do not stipulate a maximum length.

Dog harnesses must be designed to accommodate pulling forces and should have padding around the neck area. Under no circumstances should the towline be attached to the dog's collar. Your dog should not be left unattended while in harness.

Dog collars are still worn, however, and may be mandatory for all dogs for ID and proof of required vaccinations. As with any collar, it should fit snugly to prevent the dog from slipping out. A loose collar (one you can place more than two fingers under) is an invitation for a dog to slip out, especially at the starting line when two dogs connected by a neckline are jumping back and forth and throwing themselves into the harness.

Emergency leads are required to be carried by skijorers during some races. Leads are usually 5 to 7 feet long with a loop on one end and a snap on the opposite end, and are used to secure dogs to trees or other fixed objects along the trail in an emergency. One lead should be carried for each dog, since more than one dog cannot be secured with a single lead. Leads can be standard walking leashes or can be fashioned from poly rope. Bungee sections or portions of towlines do not qualify as emergency leads.

Necklines are required with multiple dogs and are used to attach a maximum of two lead dogs by the collar. An additional incentive to use necklines is that they encourage multiple dogs to travel around the same side of an obstacle. This prevents the dogs from parting at ("splitting") the obstacle and pulling the skijorer directly into the obstruction. Necklines are also used to attach the wheel dog's collar to the gangline (main pulling line).

Skijorers are encouraged to wear helmets on challenging or unfamiliar terrain, especially if new to the sport. Many skijor trails meander through densely wooded areas, sometimes passing quite close to trees and other obstacles. The terrain and travel speeds can be very similar to mountain biking, a sport in which wearing a helmet is de rigueur behavior. If you have any doubt as to whether or not you should be wearing a helmet, go easy on yourself. Wear the helmet.

The intent of race organizers is to create a positive, friendly atmosphere for all participants and spectators. Skijorers are expected to act courteously and professionally, and those who do not are at risk of being disqualified. The following rules are typical:

- Dogs should be treated humanely at all times.

- Dogs must be kept under control and separated from other dogs, unless contact is mutually agreed to by all parties involved.

- Loose dogs are not permitted on the course or in staging areas.

- Aggressive dogs are not welcome.

- Doping of any kind is prohibited for skijorer and dogs.

- Profanity is prohibited.

- Dog waste must be picked up as quickly as possible. (Note: this pertains to pre- and postrace activities. Racers are not expected to pick up dog waste while actually racing.)

- Skijorers must be careful not to interfere with or impede the progress of other racers on the course or in the staging area.

- Skijorers should offer to help injured skijorers or mushers encountered on the trail.

- Any complaints or protests should be registered with race officials in a courteous and professional manner, away from public view.

In most races you'll be given a number to wear during the race. This number must be clearly visible to race officials for purposes of validating your progress on the course and confirming final elapsed time. Failure to properly display the race number usually results in disqualification.

JACK KUNTZ

The Start

Check before the race to determine the basis for "official race time." This may vary from Greenwich Mean Time (GMT) to local conventions, such as the pocket watch carried by the official race timer. Starting times, procedures, course layout and official race time are discussed at the prerace mushers' or drivers' meeting, which is important to attend (and may be mandatory in some races). Don't hesitate to ask about any aspect of official time or starting if you have questions. Skijorers should synchronize their watches prior to race day, if possible, and the prerace meeting is the best place to do this.

Racers will be given a start time and at many races a chute time as well. Chute time is the latest time that the skijorer is expected to arrive at the staging area (near the starting line). Start time is when the skijoring team will actually begin racing on the course. Chute time is usually two or three minutes prior to start time. The interval between chute and start times is used by officials to mark participants' dogs and verify start order, and by skijorers to put on skis and other equipment. First-time racers will be amazed at how quickly two minutes expire!

Start order is usually determined by lottery. Skijorers (especially beginners) can request to opt out of the drawing in order to start at the back of the field. This provides a couple of benefits for inexperienced racers. First, it allows them to observe a number of starts before their turn, which can help demystify the process. Second, it removes much of the pressure associated with starting the race, since the more veteran racers will already be underway.

The back of the field is usually very tolerant and helpful when it comes to skijorers who are new to the sport. Spills, dogs that may not yet fully understand LET'S GO, tangled lines and so forth are frequently encountered when learning to race. The race volunteers at the starting area and on the trail (called "trail help") are helpful and supportive. Don't hesitate to ask them for assistance.

Remaining entrants are selected via random drawing: first selected starts first; second selected starts second, and so on until all positions are determined. Start order for subsequent races is determined by the finish time in the first race: fastest time starts first, second fastest time starts second, etc. Race rules will occasionally reverse this sequence.

A time bonus is sometimes awarded to the first skijorer starting each day to compensate for not having a team to chase down the trail. As discussed in Chapter 3, dogs have a profound chasing instinct and are stimulated by skijorers and dogs running ahead of them on the trail. For example, the time bonus might consist of a two-second per kilometer subtraction from the actual elapsed time. A 5k race having a two-second time bonus would result in a ten-second time reduction. A skijorer starting first in this example and posting a finishing time of 14 minutes would be given an official finishing time of 13:50. The time bonus rule is not common, though the concept has merit and deserves consideration by race planners.

Starting intervals will vary but normally are 30 seconds or one minute between teams. Race officials will use their discretion to optimize the spacing between starting teams, based on the number of racers and trail conditions.

It is important that skijorers arrive punctually at the start area, and many races will stipulate how far in advance they should arrive. Skijorers may be requested to be in the starting area a couple of minutes prior to their official start time (see previous notes on chute time). Skijorers missing their start time are penalized by having minutes added to their elapsed race time. For example, a skijorer running the course in sixteen minutes but getting a late start may be given an official time of nineteen minutes. At many races, a missed start requires skijorers to start at the very end of the field. This can be a costly penalty, since the clock starts ticking at the original start time.

You may need assistance getting from your vehicle to the starting line. If so, be sure to ask for help. Carrying your equipment behind an energetic dog while crossing a potentially slippery parking lot is not advised. Instead, carry your skis and poles over to the starting area while your dog or dogs are still in their kennels, and then return for the dogs. A note of caution: Stay alert for skijoring or mushing teams in motion when heading to the start; they may not be able to stop to avoid a person or dog cutting in front of them. Instruct any helpers you bring along to be aware of what's happening around them.

When lining up for the start, the front tips of the skijorer's skis must be positioned behind the starting line until the race official has signaled the start. The start is from a stationary or at-rest position; "flying starts" are not permitted. You'll probably need someone to help hold your dog prior to the start. The excitement at the starting line is contagious for most dogs! Many dogs will become frantic when they observe other dogs starting ahead of them down the trail and will want to join in. It is very important that you keep your dog under control during this time. Any helpers you've brought along to the race can assist. Otherwise, there are usually plenty of volunteers available.

During the Race

Once you're underway, you'll notice an immediate contrast between the commotion at the starting line and the tranquility of the trail. As you find a rhythm between your own stride and that of your dog, you may also develop an increased focus on the elements of skijoring. Your dog will be aware of the teams ahead of you and will likely be highly motivated to pursue them.

JACK KUNTZ

During the course of the race, you will almost definitely be passed by teams overtaking you from behind, pass teams that you are overtaking, or both (and probably more than once). It is important that you understand the expected behavior in passing situations.

From the beginning of the race until the last kilometer or half-mile, skijorers should pass as follows when conditions are safe:

- Skijorer doing the passing shouts "Trail!" before attempting to pass, usually about 40 feet behind the skijorer being passed. Shouting "Trail!" too early may be an unwelcome distraction to the team being passed, while shouting "Trail!" too late may not allow the skijorer being passed enough time to prepare for your pass.

- Skijorer being passed should move to right side of the trail if possible and keep team moving (dogs should not stop).

- Skijorer being passed must stop poling and hold poles behind, low and away from passing team.

- Passed skijorer must slow team slightly as passing skijorer moves ahead.

- Passing skijorer must exercise extreme caution when poling in close proximity to team being passed.

- After completion of pass, passed skijorer must maintain a minimum distance (approximately 40 feet) behind passing team to avoid distracting passing team's dogs.

- At most races, passed teams cannot attempt to repass for two kilometers or three minutes, whichever occurs first.

When your team is passed, your dogs will chase the passing team with renewed vigor. In many cases your team—if permitted—will catch up to the team that just passed. Besides being against the rules, this action slows both teams as they head towards the finish. The reason is simple: The dogs on the lead team become distracted as your dogs approach from behind. The resulting break in concentration slows their pace. By slowing your team slightly after being passed and maintaining an adequate distance, you can take advantage of the chase object in front and enjoy the ride home. Think of it as free ticket for a fast ride to the finish banner!

Assistance is usually available at various points along the race trail. No time penalty is typically levied against skijorers using trail help to resolve tangles or other problems. The skijorer is expected to provide clear instructions to any helpers when seeking assistance along the trail. Of course, trail help cannot push or pull the skijorer down the trail or physically assist in the forward progress of the team.

Trail help can also alert emergency personnel of injuries to skijorer or dog. Skijorers should promptly seek medical attention for any injuries they receive along the race course. Injuries are rare but can result in any sporting event, so race safely by staying within your speed and control comfort range.

The Finish

The homestretch (normally the last kilometer or half-mile) of the race is referred to as "No Man's Land," though our dogs prefer the term "No Dog's Land." A significant change in the rules of passing applies in this final segment of the race. Once in No Dog's Land, skijorers can pass at will whenever conditions are safe for passing. In other words, there are no restrictions on the number of passes that may be attempted, and no minimum separation distance during the last kilometer, as long as safety is not compromised. "Trail!" must still be called out prior to passing in each passing attempt, and all other passing rules apply as before.

Timing for the race ends when the dog's nose (or the nose of the first dog on the team) crosses the finish line. Skijorers must exit the chute area immediately to clear the way for subsequent finishing teams. Please do not stop and ask race officials for your race time; they will still be busy with the race. Support personnel or dog

handlers are welcome but must stay clear of other teams finishing the race.

The official finish line may be located some distance (perhaps 100 yards) before the spectator finish line. Some dogs will slow down when nearing a crowd of spectators, sensing that the race is over. The earlier official finish line gives a more consistent assessment of a team's performance.

Racing is Fun!

THOR

Racing helps shorten my learning curve. It sharpens my focus and gives me the opportunity to see a range of styles and techniques on the trail. One of the unique challenges is the juggling of numerous variables during the actual race—my speed, technique, my dog's performance and condition, using the right commands at the right time, passing other teams, weather conditions—the list goes on and on!

It's also a great opportunity to socialize with friendly, outdoor-minded people who are crazy about dogs. And it lets Spot observe other dogs performing on the trail. He's almost pure energy when the team ahead of us takes off, and he hears the "call of the wild." The atmosphere is absolutely thrilling.

Scoring is based on the lowest official elapsed time, or combination of elapsed times if multiple races are involved. This official
time will include any bonuses awarded to the team starting first for
the day in each class, if applicable.

At the Racing Venue

- Try to park in the same spot each day, to minimize
  chances of virus or parasite transmittal. If your dog is
  sick, don't put other dogs at risk of exposure by bringing
  him to the race.

- If you're a spectator at a race, leave your dog in the car or
  at home. Don't bring your dog close to the trail when
  teams are racing.

- ▶ If spectating, feel free to volunteer to help skijorers or mushers participating in the race. If offering assistance, ask them first if they need help and then ask exactly what they would like you to do. Do this before approaching or assisting the team.

- ▶ Stay alert when near skijor or mushing teams in motion, especially in parking and staging areas or where they might approach you from behind. They require time to stop or change direction.

- ▶ Enjoy the sights, sounds and action!

The following excerpt is from Thor's skijoring journal, describing his very first race. It highlights several common mistakes and misunderstandings of newcomers to the sport. It also contains valuable insights for beginners and potential racers alike, and can be of interest whether or not the reader intends to compete in a race or be an informed spectator. Thor's blunders in his first race remind us that even able competitors come from humble beginnings.

THOR's First Race

The first skijor race I entered was held in association with a dog-sled race near a small resort town. The race was a popular one, with nearly 150 mushers and 40 skijorers in attendance. I had run 10k races and had bike-raced for years, and felt I had a good understanding of how to prepare for this kind of race. In fact, since I was in great shape and had top-notch dogs in Spot and Bowser, I even thought I had a shot at winning the event.

The venue for the morning race was about an hour from my house, so I roused the dogs early to feed them and allow plenty of time for them to digest their breakfast. I hadn't allowed for this change in their routine, however, and shouldn't have been surprised at their lack of appetite at this early hour. I thought, OK, I'll outsmart you guys, and I grabbed a pound of hamburger from the fridge. Within minutes the kitchen was filled with the aroma of frying beef, as I proceeded to cook up a "carnivore's delight" breakfast, at 5:00 A.M.! Never mind that this was far too much food—at least they wolfed it down.

I had missed the prerace mushers' meeting the previous evening, due to a conflict. Not my preference, of course, but I figured other skijorers could give me a quick summary of the details covered. I didn't realize at the time that vital information about the course, official race time, and start order is shared at this meeting. I would learn about this later. I decided to play it safe and set my watch to Greenwich Mean Time (GMT), since surely this would be the most accurate means for the race administrators to ensure a synchronized start. Little did I know that GMT is rarely if ever used, that the local time is usually announced at the mushers' meeting as the official race time.

I parked in the race lot and began my preparations for the race. I let the dogs out so they could do their business, but to no avail, so I returned them to their kennels inside the van. They were so excited by all the noise and commotion that they couldn't even consider such routine functions. Our start time was still over an hour and a half away, so I had plenty of time to scope things out. An announcer's voice boomed over the portable public address system, calling out start times by class, musher and skijorer names; race sponsors; trail updates and conditions; and other last-minute pieces of information. Clusters of lycra-clad skijorers mingled with dogs and spectators as equipment was laid out and inspected. The parking lot was a sea of howling animals, and should have been labeled a "barking lot." I roamed freely and chatted with other racers, mushers and dog owners before I realized that I needed to continue preparing in earnest for the start of the race. Now I know to do my preparations first, chatting last.

I returned and let the dogs out of the van so they could try again to answer nature's call, but still no luck. They had absolutely no interest in such matters. The sights, sounds, smells and constant flurry of activity that surrounded us had them completely overwhelmed.

It should be noted for the uninitiated that it is essential that your dog relieve himself prior to starting a race. Failure to obey this basic law will result in problems during the race, guaranteed. One can imagine the disappointment of coming into the homestretch, neck and neck with a competing team, only to have your dog come to a complete stop and begin to defecate, perhaps 20 yards from the finish line. For most solo dogs, no amount of encouragement will persuade them to interrupt their business once they have started, and so you would likely watch the competing team sail unchallenged across the finish line. Dogs running in a group are less likely to be able to stop during the run to relieve themselves, since the rest of the group will pull them along.

In what I thought was a flash of brilliance, I decided to pack up the dogs and drive to a remote, quiet location to encourage them to conclude their business. An open field several miles away proved suitable for the occasion, but now we were playing our own version of "Beat the Clock" since this action chewed up precious additional minutes. I let the dogs out of their kennels and waited for them to perform. Instead, they both faced the direction of the starting line, eyes focused on the horizon from which the intriguing though barely discernable sounds emanated. They obviously weren't sure why they were here and not there, and after a minute I began to wonder as well. My mind drifted, and all I could think about was the myriad of prerace tasks that I still needed to complete: sort through and organize equipment; put the harnesses on the dogs; pin on my race number; arrive at the starting line on time; and so on. And I was by myself, without anyone else to hold the dogs and assist. Suddenly I was back in the present, as nature finally intervened and our mission was accomplished. We returned in haste to the prerace barking lot.

At this point I noticed that the air temperature was actually pretty cold. I had been wearing my racing clothes, which are sleek and aerodynamic, but not excessively warm when one is standing around in a parking lot. I made a mental note to wear an extra layer or jacket during the prerace period—one that could be removed immediately prior to the start. As I scanned the parking lot to see what other skijorers were wearing, I noticed that most were well into their pre-race preparations and some were even heading to the start.

A quick glance at my watch confirmed my worst suspicion: time was evaporating fast and we had less than 15 minutes to make our chute time. It's interesting how panic manifests itself in the human psyche at times like these. On the positive side it can become a catalyst for quick, decisive action; on the negative, it hinders clear thought and confuses the afflicted, greatly increasing the time required to perform even routine tasks. Unfortunately, as the panic coursed through my veins, my effectiveness suffered.

Instead of quickly pinning on my race number, my numb fingers fumbled the safety pins, and two dropped to the snow. Flustered, I proceeded to mix up my dogs' harnesses, and put Spot's on Bowser and Bowser's on Spot. As I frantically tried to correct my mistakes and prepare for our departure, I could clearly hear the tick-tock of an imaginary, yet omnipresent clock.

After fastening my skijor belt and connecting the towline, I realized that I needed to begin my trip to the start area if I were going to have any chance of starting on time. I knew that arriving at the starting line at just the right time is crucial. Arrive too early and one is faced with rambunctious dogs viewing the ordeal as a date with a launching pad, clearly primed for immediate liftoff. Besides being a hassle, this results in dogs wasting precious energy before the race even starts. Arrive too late and the skijorer is assessed a time penalty or is required to start last.

I hooked up the dogs, and we prepared to cruise to the start. As Murphy would predict, my dogs immediately crossed their lines and wrapped around the front of the van. I managed to get them unwrapped and ready to go. Next, Spot pulled out of his collar, as I evidently had not made sure it was tight enough. I was hoping no one was watching as Bowser paraded around flaunting the neck-

line, still attached to an empty collar! Getting Spot set up again consumed more valuable time.

I didn't realize how slick the parking lot was, especially when attempting to navigate it with my dogs hitched up, while walking in my ski boots and carrying skis and poles. In an instant my dogs took off, pulling my feet out from underneath me and dragging me across the parking lot on my posterior. The first time this happened I foolishly declined the offer of assistance from a friendly bystander, but when I went down a second time I gladly accepted his offer. I would learn later that most racers make a separate trip to the starting chute with their skis and poles, and then return for their dogs.

When I finally arrived at the starting chute, I was baffled by the puzzled glance given me by the starting official. She informed me that I had missed my chute time, and would be required to start last. So much for using GMT to set my watch—guess I should've been at the mushers' meeting.

Finally it was almost time for us to begin the race. With helpers holding my dogs, I strapped on my skis and prepared for the countdown. I should note that without the volunteers and helpers present at these races, there would be no way to properly stage such events. On many occasions I received their helpful assistance, and now was no different. The decibel level at the start was absolutely deafening as dogs voiced their primordial support for the activity they were about to begin. Dogs simply can't stand the sight of other dogs starting ahead of them and vanishing down the trail. My dogs were going wild, after several hours of anticipating this moment. 5-4-3-2-1-LET'S GO!

However, an instant before the start, my glasses fogged up. When wearing a face mask, you shouldn't put your glasses on until the last possible moment. I reached to pull them up and in doing so, straightened my knees and shifted my position. The change in tension was instantly transmitted to the dogs, who reacted by adjusting their forward pull. Subtle changes, but as we started I was slightly off balance, and when we came rocketing out of the starting gate, I struggled mightily to maintain my balance. I didn't anticipate the extraordinary force that two dogs can produce, upon hearing LET'S GO.

The snow was crusty and the surface was rutted immediately out of the chute, caused by heavy and intense use. I didn't lean forward fast enough; I fell back and then overcorrected as we picked up speed. For 20 yards I fought to regain my balance, with arms flailing wildly. I lost the battle and went sprawling into the snow, executing an inglorious swan dive. Of course my dogs continued to pull while I was down, making it difficult to get back up. Not only was this an ominous way to start the race; it was also in front of several hundred spectators, providing me a free lesson in humility.

The impact cracked my ski binding, but a hasty inspection indicated that it might still function well enough to continue. After picking myself up, I figured there was no longer much to lose, and I concentrated on simply salvaging whatever I could of the race. Soon we hit our stride. My initial sensation of embarrassment gave way to relief and ultimately to awe as we established a rhythm and began gaining ground on other skijorers. This was my first real taste of skijor racing, and it was magnificent. In fact, I remember thinking the first half-mile was the most fun I'd ever had, that we were poetry in motion.

However, the event wasn't over just yet, and I realized I still had to navigate a challenging course filled with other skijorers and their dogs. As we moved to pass a team we were overtaking, I absent-mindedly gave my dogs the GEE instead of HAW command, causing them to dart off track and become tangled with the dogs being passed. This was entirely my fault, but fortunately the other skijorer was most courteous, and we managed to untangle the mess. I held my dogs back while he resumed racing.

Once again, we resumed moving and picked up momentum. Beautiful, I thought, as I started drinking in the scenery, sounds and smells. Perhaps I relaxed a bit too much, and that contributed to my catching a ski tip. Things happen fast at 20 mph—skis can move sideways in a split second, requiring constant vigilance and concentration.

JACK KUNTZ

Instantly, I went down again, rolling and tangling in the lines while my dogs probably wondered whose side I was on. I had blown out of one of my skis. I spotted it stuck in the snow, ten feet behind me. The problem was that my dogs were pulling their lines taut, and I couldn't get back to retrieve my ski. Try as I might, it was no use—Bowser and Spot were not going to relent. I took off my other ski and was able to get enough traction to pull the dogs back to where I could reach the ski. Of course, they thought I had gone insane, pulling them the wrong direction on a trail that we had been flying down a few moments earlier. In hindsight, I wish I had known and used the COME AROUND command; that would've made life much easier.

I hurried to put my skis back on so that we could resume the race. I had just stepped into the first binding when another team came hurtling by. My dogs made an independent determination that this was their cue, and they immediately took off in pursuit. WHOA! NO! WHOA! I cried, as I hobbled along with one ski on and one ski off, while trying again to resist their potent forward tug. Perhaps pity for their battle-scarred leader influenced them at this point; in any case, they relaxed the line tension just enough so that I could again pull them back, grab the elusive ski and get us back in the race.

For the rest of the event, I recall being much more aware of all

the potential small occurrences that could trigger larger mishaps, and staying much more focused on the race. I still allowed myself to savor the sheer beauty of it all, but I couldn't let my mind wander from the present. We didn't win that day, but I considered the race a complete success anyway, not only because we made it through a number of miscues but also because we ran well and gained considerable ground on the leaders. I thought to myself, "How often can one be gratified, humbled, encouraged, frustrated and awestruck in less than an hour?"

CHAPTER NINE

The Warm-Weather Alternatives: Canicross, Bikejoring, Rollerjoring

Unless you live at a high elevation or near Ernest Shackleton's route through the Weddell Sea near Antarctica, you likely won't have access to snow-covered skijor trails for more than perhaps five months a year. This is actually a great opportunity to extend to another dimension the partnership that you've nurtured with your dog. Three of the most common alternatives are covered here—canicross, bikejoring, and rollerjoring. Bikejoring, the most obviously named of the three, is simply the combination of bicycling with skijoring. While conceptually straightforward, it can be quite challenging in practice. The tips and details included here will help you enjoy the experience of hooking up your dog to your bike.

Canicross, a European term for running your dog in harness as you run behind, is gaining in popularity in North America. Canicross allows you to continue conditioning both yourself and your dogs, yet has enough variation from winter skijoring to provide variety and challenge. Rollerjoring is inline skating or rollerskiing behind your dog. Dog-powered sports such as these fall under the category of canisports or dry-land mushing.

JOHN SANDBERG

Canicross

Canicross is skijoring without snow. The skijorer can use the same belt, and the dog the same harness. This is a profound improvement over running your dog off to the side with a leash, as many runners have attempted at one time or another. Switching the leash from one hand to the other disrupts the runner's rhythm, provides no shock absorption or slack line alleviation, and can produce high lateral forces. Sore arm, neck and shoulder muscles are often the result when your dog pulls while you're holding the leash. Canicross reduces these problems by freeing you from holding the leash and providing shock absorption in the line.

The standard skijoring towline can be used for canicross, though care must be taken since it will be longer than needed for running behind your dog. The standard skijoring line length was designed for a skier, and thus includes three or four feet of line that is unnecessary when running. This extra length can have you jumping over slack rope or getting wrapped up with your dog if you're not vigilant. Worse, it allows your dog increased range to run in front of pedestrian, bicycle or vehicle traffic. The extra length is not needed because your reaction time is quicker on foot, and your speed is lower. Using your winter skijoring equipment without modification requires that you keep one hand available to control the line.

A better solution is to shorten the towline for canicross, assuming your towline consists of two pieces: a bungee section and a tug section. Simply remove the tugline and put the bronze snap on the end of the bungee section. This should leave a line that is about five feet in length. The belt strap or bridle on most skijor belts adds another foot or so, giving a total length of about six feet from your waist to the back of your dog's harness. This keeps your dog far enough ahead to avoid running into her, yet close enough to maintain control with a quick reel-in.

A separate towline designed specifically for canicross is also available. Canicross lines are shorter and often have a built-in loop handle for keeping your dog close and secure when necessary. Features include reflective braiding for nighttime runs and a large connecting loop where it attaches to the belt, permitting the line to double as a leash for traditional dog walks.

If you've skijored before, the transition to canicross will be simple. You don't have to worry about crossing your ski tips, hitting your dog's hind legs with a ski or slipping on an icy trail. And less equipment makes it easier to hit the trail—no skis, poles, boots, wax or cold-weather clothing required. Your dog may still require booties, however, so refer to the Equipment chapter for de-

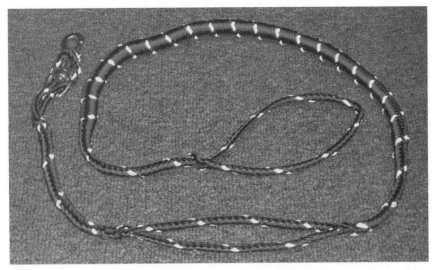

Reflective canicross line with braided handle

tails about the use of booties. While speed and exhilaration suffer a bit in comparison to skijoring, canicross is still a great way to keep in shape and train with your dog.

Canicross is recommended for those who have not yet attempted skijoring. As mentioned, since you're free of the ski aspects of the sport, you can focus on working with your dog and practicing commands. Once you and your dog are kindred spirits regarding trail running and are familiar with GEE and HAW, adding snow and skis becomes much easier.

Several intriguing aspects of canicross are noted here, and you may discover your own additions to this list. "Hands-free" running with your dog permits better balance and control, and allows the natural back-and-forth arm carry motion of running without a dog. The extra help on uphill portions of your route will be an absolute thrill if you're used to solo jogging. And the relative abundance of dog-walking trails or quiet roads in most areas means you'll have many trail options to choose from.

Cautionary Notes for Canicross

Start with a single dog. If you have two or more dogs, always try canicross first with just one dog. Canicross with two or more dogs on downhill sections can be perilous.

JOHN SANDBERG

Adjust the belt lower. The skijor belt should be placed slightly lower on your hips than for skijoring. In skijoring, when your dog lunges forward your skis slide forward and the force is softened. However, in canicross, your feet are planted and so the force is transmitted more directly to your body. Placing the belt lower helps mitigate this effect by transferring force from your back to your hips. You should also be ready to assume a ski tuck position by bending forward at the waist so that your back is nearly parallel to the ground (see "Safety Tips and Procedures" at the beginning of Chapter 3). Leading equipment vendors now offer multistage bungees to help absorb much of this shock.

Bring the right equipment. Canicross requires less equipment, but there are a few important items to consider. Eyewear is always important, because your dog can kick up dirt, gravel, woodchips, etc. And booties for your dog can be critical on hard road surfaces or rocky trails.

Maintain traction and control on downhill sections. Your dog should respond to EASY and WHOA, or you will likely end up throwing the "parachute brake" (i.e., sitting down). When skijoring, you can snowplow to reduce downhill speed, but in canicross you are limited to resisting or braking with your feet. This can be precarious on slick or loose gravel trails, dewy grass or other surfaces where traction is not ideal. Even on good trails, remember that your footing will not be as solid when a dog is pulling you on downward slopes.

Minimize potential for overheating. Canicross is typically done in temperatures above freezing, so be cognizant of your dog's need for water and limited heat tolerance. Remember that dogs don't sweat, they pant, so don't hesitate to let your dog take a quick break in the lake on warmer days. Make sure that you have plenty of water available for your dog and yourself before, during and after your run. Run in the cooler morning or evening hours, and choose a tree-shaded trail if the sun is directly overhead. Keep the run short if it's a warm day.

Cool down properly. On a warm day, the time immediately following your run is critical for your dog; this is when body temperatures can soar. Your dog must have shade, air flow and cool but not ice-cold water. Never leave your dog alone after a warm-weather workout until you're certain that she has cooled down properly. If you drove to the trail, crack your windows or turn on the air conditioning for the ride home.

Know and control your top speed. Be careful not to exceed a comfortable speed on any section of your route. While this concern is not unique to canicross, the difference here is that you're not gliding on skis, rollerblades or bike but running on your own two legs. You may recall from your youth what happened when, for whatever reason, you began running faster than your legs could comfortably transport you. Your stride quickens and then lengthens as you begin taking huge, out-of-control steps to maintain the pace. Controlling your speed and knowing your limits will help avoid injury to you and your dog.

Increase distance gradually. Don't attempt a 10k run on your first canicross outing. Start with small, manageable excursions and then ratchet up gradually. This approach provides conditioning and endurance training for both dog and human. Gauge your dog's reaction to heat and monitor his pad and toenail wear.

Canicross is a great way to hit the trail with your dog for an invigorating workout. This versatile sport is enjoyed by veterans that appreciate its "anywhere, anytime" characteristics. It is also recommended for beginners because it is the least challenging of the warm-weather alternatives and requires the smallest amount of equipment. Persons accustomed to running their dog on a leash will probably develop an immediate fondness for canicross.

Bikejoring

If you're already comfortable with skijoring, or if you've had success with canicross, you might consider bikejoring. This qualification sequence is deliberate; bikejoring is exhilarating but can quickly test all your skills, including bicycling competency! Adding dogs to the cycling equation changes the handling characteristics of the bicycle and introduces an element of unpredictability. The point here is not to discourage bikejoring, but to suggest that aspiring bikejorers become comfortable with each of the elements first, especially controlling a dog while in motion.

Exercise for Bikejorer and Dog?

Bikejoring, unlike skijoring and canicross, is probably better for exercising and training your dog rather than providing a workout

JOHN SANDBERG

for yourself. Bikejoring is excellent for strong or fast dogs that prefer to go faster or longer than you are able to run. Because at least light tension must be applied to the towline at all times, the bikejorer is often required to feather (smoothly apply) the brakes rather than pedal for most of the outing. The towline tension is necessary to avoid tangles with the front wheel, which can cause a crash.

In certain conditions, however, it is possible to enjoy a challenging workout while bikejoring. For example, a hilly trail requires a bikejorer to pedal hard up the climbs, especially if bikejoring with one dog on a steep grade. Moreover, grassy, sandy or wood chip trails can require significant pedaling input from the bikejorer even on flat sections. This is due to the increased rolling resistance these surfaces create versus trail surfaces like asphalt or concrete, which should be avoided when possible. Long runs on hard surfaces can cause pad, toenail and impact stress to your dog's legs and joints.

Importance of Control

The key to successful training in any dog-powered sport is control, and this responsibility rests 100% with the bikejorer. As with driving a car, loss of control can occur at any speed and depends more on conditions and circumstances than on absolute speed. If control is compromised, the probability of a mishap increases exponentially. The main risk factor is excessive speed for any given situation, as opposed to maximum speed. To illustrate, a bikejorer may have complete control of his or her team at 20 mph on a straight and flat trail, but on a downhill section with a difficult turn, 9 mph may be too fast.

The choice of bicycle has a tremendous influence on control. A mountain bike is designed for off-road use and is best suited for all-around bikejoring. A good quality mountain bike can bring a powerful dog team to a standstill quickly and safely, allowing the bikejorer to stay within his or her comfort range at all times. Experience is, of course, a critical component of the control equation, but beginners and seasoned cyclists alike should start with a dependable mountain bike. Road bikes (i.e., bikes with narrow, high-pressure tires, caliper brakes and no front suspension) are not recommended for bikejoring.

Octagonal Encounters of the Worst Kind

THOR

Out of the driveway and we're on our way! Helga is out front rollerblading to get a head start, and I'm sailing behind on my bike holding the dogs' leashes. I forgot the neckline, but it doesn't seem to be affecting the dogs at all. They're staying together and running so fast that it's a challenge braking with one hand.

Normally I'd connect the dogs directly to my bike, but today I'm only out for a quick ride around the neighborhood. Holding the leashes in one hand is a bit tricky, but I'm short on time and the dogs are anxious to go. In the rush to gather equipment I forget to strap on my helmet.

Helga is a block or so ahead and moving at a good clip, so we quicken the pace to catch her receding form. In no time at all we've accelerated to 20 mph. As I simultaneously negotiate the pavement, monitor the dogs and use my left hand to control the dogs' leashes, I notice a loose dog running off to the side. Looking over, I breathe a sigh of relief as I watch the dog stop at the edge of his yard. When I return my attention to the road, there it is, right in front of me in bold letters: STOP. The dogs have already gone around the sign; however, Bowser went to the left, Spot to the right.

A moment later, my right handlebar catches the stop sign, stopping the bike immediately. As Sir Isaac Newton predicted years ago, a body in motion tends to remain in motion, unless acted upon by another force. I am thus treated to both of these aspects of Newtonian mechanics. First I'm catapulted over my handlebars, on the verge of becoming an airborne projectile traveling at 20 mph. But my brief flirtation with zero gravity is immediately interrupted by

Equipment for Bikejoring

As with skijoring or canicross, one of the benefits of bikejoring is that equipment needs are relatively modest. You'll need a basic mountain bike as indicated above, but beyond that you should be able to use your skijoring or canicross gear with minimal modifications. The following section highlights important characteristics of the equipment required for bikejoring.

Mountain Bike

Off-road knobby tires

Good traction is essential in bikejoring, especially on hilly trails with loose or wet surfaces. Choose good quality tires that have pro-

another force—that of the (now stationary) left handlebar on my bike. Catching me a couple inches from my groin, it deflects my forward motion and causes me to flip in midair. Apparently, most of my momentum has been transferred to a brand new 3-inch bruise that fortunately missed strategic areas, but nevertheless takes about a month to fully heal.

As I roll over on the ground several times and eventually sit up, the dogs stop and return, once again confirming the value of discipline and training. I'm dazed and bruised, but otherwise intact as I look towards the diminishing figure of Helga moving down the street. At that moment an elderly lady who happens to be motoring by stops, rolls down her window, and asks "are you all right?" I nod and thank her, get up, gather my dogs and hobble over to inspect my bike. Having seen the entire incident, she isn't so sure, but continues on. A couple of blocks later she pulls alongside Helga. "A man back there had a terrible bicycle accident," she intones to Helga, who of course immediately reverses direction and speeds to the scene.

In retrospect, I was lucky. I had made several foolish mistakes on this outing. First, a helmet should always be worn, period. Accidents can happen on quick trips or at slow speeds, and it's also tough to predict what challenges you'll encounter on your ride. Second, the dogs should be attached to the bicycle, not held on a leash, to free up both hands for steering and braking. Next, if running with more than one dog, always assume that they will pass on opposite sides of an obstacle. This assumption will allow you to prepare for the situation by issuing commands (such as GEE OVER), slowing down, or stopping entirely. Finally, a neckline is recommended when running two dogs side by side in dual lead. The neckline connects both dogs at the collar and reduces the odds that they'll "split" an obstacle on the trail.

truding knobs, and match the tread type with the type of trails you'll encounter most frequently. For example, there are tires manufactured specifically for loose gravel, mud, hard packed dirt, sand, etc. Your local bike shop can help you select the correct tires.

Avoid semi-slick tires, which are designed for low rolling resistance rather than maximum traction. If you are running two or three dogs, consider mounting your tires backwards (opposite the directional arrow) to increase tread bite while braking. For improved grip, inflate your tires to the middle to lower end of the suggested range to expand the amount of tire contacting the trail. The lower inflation will also provide a smoother ride and greater control on bumpy or loose trail surfaces.

Good quality brakes and knobby tires are essential for bikejoring.

"Stop-on-a-dime" brakes

A good set of tires is ineffective if paired with mediocre quality brakes. Recent innovations in the mountain bike industry have significantly improved braking systems. These new designs generate impressive stopping force with only light hand pressure, one of the key reasons mountain bikes are recommended for bikejoring.

Referred to as V-brakes, the design allows a bikejorer to control one or more dogs on a challenging trail without concern for hand cramps. However, not all V-brakes are created equal, so go for a test ride and practice simulated hard stops and braking on downhill sections before hooking up your dog to the bike. Check with your bike shop for possible modification or replacement of your brakes. And if you bikejor often in wet conditions, such as on dewy morning runs or in melting frost, exchange the standard issue brake pads for wet-weather versions. As a side benefit, the wet-weather versions often eliminate brake pad chatter and screeching.

One cautionary note for hard-core bikejorers running two or three powerful dogs on a frequent basis: inspect your rims occasionally for excessive wear, which can manifest as hairline cracks on the rim sidewall. If you bikejor frequently in wet, sandy conditions, a set of rims will last one to two seasons. The brake friction and grit simply wears through the rim surface. Ceramic treated rims are more durable and stop better in wet conditions but wear through brake pads faster than do smooth anodized rims.

Mountain bike manufacturers have recently begun adding disc brakes to many of their new models. Disc brakes have been used on downhill racers' bikes for years, but now are becoming mainstream on cross-country-style mountain bikes. Downhill racers usually prefer disc brakes for their dependable braking at high speeds and performance in extreme conditions.

Good quality disc brakes are superior to V-brakes in stopping power and modulation, but tend to be more expensive and technologically complex. Numerous designs employ hydraulic systems similar to those found in cars, although newer, simpler mechanical versions function well and are gaining popularity. Disc brakes are usually purchased as original equipment on a new bike due to the high cost of retrofitting an older bike.

Finally, disc brakes use a pad and rotor combination at the center of the wheel rather than a standard bicycle brake at the rim. This eliminates friction and wear at the rim sidewall, an important improvement for bikejorers. Another benefit is wet-weather performance, where disc brakes significantly outperform all other bicycle braking systems.

In summary, a mountain bike with knobby tires and either good quality V-brakes or disc brakes will allow you to stop quickly under most trail conditions.

Front suspension

Mountain bikes are usually equipped with front shock suspension. Front-end suspension minimizes the impact of rough terrain and improves handling and control for off-road riding. Front suspension allows the bikejorer to brake constantly without his or her hands bouncing off the handlebars; during braking, only the thumb and palm contact the handlebar. Front suspension also improves control by keeping the tire in contact with the ground instead of bouncing over bumpy terrain. This continual contact with the trail surface also enhances traction.

Optional equipment

A front suspension mountain bike is adequate for getting started with bikejoring. The following options can further improve performance and comfort.

Most mountain bike manufacturers offer several *dual suspension* models that include a suspension fork in front and a swing arm and shock in back. Dual suspension bikes are phenomenal for bikejoring but are more expensive than models with just one shock. The advantages of control, traction and comfort, however, may be worth the expense if you plan to bikejor frequently on off-road trails. If you plan to purchase a dual suspension model, choose one with disc brakes for the ultimate bikejoring machine. You might also consider modifying your current "hardtail" (front suspension only) bike by purchasing an add-on suspension seat post to smooth out the bumps and improve traction.

Beginners and those who bikejor often on challenging trails with two or three dogs will appreciate a *quick-release seat binder*. This piece of equipment is similar to the quick-release skewers found on bicycle hubs, and allows for quick seat height adjustment at the trailhead without using tools. Experienced bikejorers often lower their bicycle seats for improved stability and handling. Dropping the seat lowers a bikejorer's center of gravity and allows the bikejorer to stand flat-footed over the seat during starts and stops. The lower position also makes it easier to steady the bike through corners by dragging a foot and reduces the possibility of flipping over the handlebars when bikejoring on steep descents. For beginners, a lowered seat simply makes bikejoring easier. Though pedaling efficiency is compromised, the tradeoff is worthwhile until the bikejorer gains experience and confidence. After finishing a bikejoring run, the seat can be quickly returned to its normal height for regular riding.

Finally, if you plan to bikejor in wet conditions, or especially in wet and cold conditions, *fenders* are an indispensable accessory.

Dog Harness

The importance of a good quality dog harness cannot be overemphasized. Never use your dog's collar for pulling! As a general rule, good quality harnesses are not available at many pet stores, which tend to carry walking- or recreational-style harnesses. Instead, go to a skijoring or mushing supplier for a harness designed for pulling. X-Back harnesses are recommended; they cradle a dog's back and sides without inhibiting running movement or chest expansion. A good quality harness should have dense padding around the neck opening and chest plate to properly distribute pulling forces. For a more detailed discussion on harnesses and proper fit, which is critically important, refer to "Equipment," Chapter 6.

The skijoring belt is *not* used when bikejoring, since doing so can interfere with steering and reduce stability. Instead, the towline is attached directly to the bicycle, as described later in this section.

Towline

No piece of bikejoring equipment works harder than the bungee towline. During starts, the bungee elongates to compensate for the dog's enthusiasm and the bikejorer's transition to speed; during running, the bungee stretches and retracts with each movement the dog and bikejorer make; during climbing and descending, the bungee works constantly to help equalize the speed between dog and bikejorer; and during braking, the bungee elongates to cushion the stopping force against the dog.

Bungee lines smooth out the bikejoring experience for your dog, allowing her to concentrate on pulling rather than anticipating when the next line jerk will occur. Bungees can also take up a significant amount of line slack, similar to the way a retractable leash winds up excess cord. This recoiling action reduces the probability of a line tangle with the front wheel or your dog's hind legs. Tangles can occur on hilly trails or when your dog slows toward the end of a run. "Equipment," Chapter 6, contains additional detail on bungee arrangements and construction.

Eye Protection

Dogs can kick up a significant amount of gravel, sand, wood chips, grass and clumps of mud while bikejoring, especially when the trail is wet. Your knobby tires will also contribute to the onslaught of flying debris. Protect your eyes by wearing a quality pair of impact resistant glasses, and if bikejoring in the woods, use clear or light-colored lenses to improve visibility.

Helmet

A helmet is mandatory equipment for bikejoring. The potential for increased speeds, variability of traction, and trees or other objects close to the trail make donning a helmet a wise decision. Dogs may bolt off-trail after rabbits at the exact moment a bikejorer is off-balance; towlines tangle the instant a bikejorer waves to a friendly passerby; humans have been known to say GEE when they mean HAW. If in doubt, remember that Murphy's Law applies equally well to bikejoring. Wear your helmet.

Booties

Your dog's feet are subject to the same stresses and abrasive forces experienced in skijoring and canicross, depending on the trail surface. The lack of a white, snowy background makes it difficult to spot bleeding from paws and requires increased vigilance over pad and toenail condition. And stretches over pavement or asphalt may also signal a need for booties. Chapter 6 contains more detail about booties.

Side-Mount Attachments

As with skijoring, not every dog will stay in front like an Iditarod veteran. If your dog isn't a dependable front runner, you may opt for a side-mount attachment (SMA). An SMA keeps the dog at the side of the bicycle via a short leash and spring mechanism that attaches to the bicycle seat tube or other part of the bike, depending on the SMA manufacturer. Because no line can tangle with the front wheel, the system is safer for exercising dogs that aren't yet ready for regular bikejoring. Bikejorers on city streets will also appreciate the short lead and greater control.

Side-mount attachment

One disadvantage of SMAs, however, is the wider swath created when bikejorer and dog travel side-by-side. On most trails this isn't a factor, but for narrow single track the traditional bikejoring setup is preferred. (See "Getting Started" and the sections following.) Another disadvantage of the SMA involves positioning. In skijoring, canicross and bikejoring, it is necessary for your dog to be in front as the leader. Since this behavior is critical for success in all three sports, it's best to reinforce the front-running leadership role whenever your dog is working, i.e., wearing the harness. In contrast, an SMA keeps your dog in a heeling, nonleading position at your side. Finally, depending on leash length and harness style, it is possible for your dog to make contact with the front wheel.

Bikejoring Variation: Scootering or Scooterjoring

Scooters have recently become popular for bikejoring. They are simple in design, fun to ride and make sense for many different trail situations, with the exception of steep climbs. Mountain bikes work better for this scenario, due to the ability of the bikejorer to smoothly add power up the hill by pedaling. Conversely, bikejorers on scooters must dismount and run or assist their dog by kicking. Both of these alternatives are distracting to a dog, the latter creating slack in the line at the very moment the dog is pulling with maximum effort.

If you're planning to purchase a scooter, select one that is designed for off-road use. Off-road scooters tend to have knobby tires and the higher ground clearances necessary for scootering off the beaten path. Additionally, many off-road versions are fitted with suspension forks, which add stability and comfort in bumpy terrain. This is important because a bumpy ride on a scooter can literally bounce the rider off the machine. To avoid being jettisoned, bend your knees and use your legs as shock absorbers.

Weight is also an important issue when considering a scooter. Extra-heavy-duty models handle sluggishly on technical trails and are difficult to push or kick uphill. Furthermore, they add to your momentum on downhills, making it more challenging to slow down. On these heavier models, the braking system and tires are critically important. If you're purchasing a new scooter, choose a model that is roughly the weight of a good quality mountain bike. Heavier versions should be purchased only if you plan to do all your scootering on relatively flat trails or will be running three or more dogs at once.

Even if you're planning to scooter the majority of the time on paved surfaces, an off-road scooter model is preferred over a city or road version. The off-road model transitions well to paved bike paths, sidewalks, streets, etc., whereas the city scooter encounters

Off-road scooter

difficulty making the crossover to off-road. The primary reason is traction. City models generally have smoother tires, which provide inadequate traction on grass, sand, dirt or gravel trails. Moreover, smooth tires have even less traction when conditions are wet. This is of paramount importance when encountering morning dew on grassy, hilly trails.

Ground clearance is also a factor, with the off-road scooter having larger wheels (usually 20 inches) and a higher foot platform. This design element is important for scootering in the city as well, given the potential for encountering obstructions such as speed bumps or curbs. The only disadvantages of the off-road scooter for city use are a slightly higher center of gravity and a small amount of vibration and noise generated by the knobby tires. The higher center of gravity should be kept in mind when cornering but is negligible in most situations. And the tire noise can be remedied by simply changing tires if you plan to scooter exclusively on paved surfaces.

Most importantly, regardless of the scooter design you choose, make sure you select a model with good quality brakes on both wheels. V-brakes, an innovation borrowed from the mountain bike industry and covered previously, are an excellent choice. With minimal hand pressure, they exert a tremendous amount of stopping power to the rim. However, V-brakes vary in performance, so test ride your scooter before buying. If the brakes can't stop you quickly on a test ride, they'll never stop you when your dog is pulling!

The V-brake design discussed earlier will keep your hands from cramping on extended runs and allow you to control your dogs effectively on downhill sections. If you scooter often in wet conditions, consider purchasing a set of wet-weather brake pad replacements for your V-brakes. They stop more effectively than standard brake pads when wet and still wear reasonably well in dry conditions.

Bikejoring: Getting Started

As mentioned during the bikejoring introduction, beginners are encouraged to have some experience running dogs before attempting bikejoring. It's also beneficial for the bikejoring dog to have experience pulling in the harness, whether in front of a runner, skijorer or dogsled. An inexperienced dog will often attempt to stay close to the owner and bike, making starting difficult. If you're new to dog powered sports, we suggest reviewing the "Teaching Your

Dog to Pull" section in Chapter 3 before reading further. Reread "Commands," Chapter 4, as well.

A successful bikejoring outing requires some planning if you're a first-timer. Practice putting the harness on your dog a time or two at home, and connect the towline to your bike before your maiden voyage. The objective here is to confirm that the line doesn't interfere with your steering capability or the safe operation of your front brake.

Connecting Towline to Bike

As mentioned previously, you should leave your skijoring belt at home when bikejoring. Wearing the belt while riding creates a myriad of problems; for example, the attached towline can tangle

Recommended— towline looped around head tube

Recommended— towline looped around spacers beneath handlebar stem

Not recommended— towline looped around end of handlebar stem

Dangerous—towline restricts front brake operation, contacts reflector

with the handlebars, brake levers, shifters, etc. Additionally, if your dog darts off-trail, the towline can travel across your handlebars and pull against your arm with significant force, compromising your balance and ability to steer. Finally, being tethered to your dog near traffic can also be a concern. Instead, connect the towline to the head tube of your bike or base of the handlebar stem, as described below.

The head tube is the forwardmost frame member located between the fork and handlebar stem. It is an excellent connecting point for the towline, since it is stationary and independent from the bicycle's steering mechanism. Furthermore, the head tube offers a relatively low fulcrum point, which reduces the amount of leverage your dog can exert from the side. This is a subtle but important advantage when your dog sojourns off-trail. A lower connecting point of even a few inches can make a significant difference in stability.

Most bike manufacturers route the front brake cable to the side of the head tube. This makes it possible to wrap the towline around the head tube without interfering with the cable or operation of the front brake. With some bikes, however, this is not possible. For example, older model bikes with M-style center-pull brakes have front brake cables that are positioned and fixed directly in front of the head tube. Bikejorers with this arrangement must wrap the towline around the handlebar stem instead.

If your front brake cable configuration allows you to connect directly to the head tube, wrap the towline around the head tube and thread the snap through the loop to create a slipknot. Make sure the knot can rotate freely from side to side to compensate for your dog's turning radius, and test your front brake to confirm that the towline doesn't restrict its operation. This is *very important*. At this time you should also verify that the towline doesn't interfere with the other cables at the front of the bike when rotated from side to side. Simply stated, the towline should be routed through the cables so that it doesn't interfere with steering or braking.

Bikejorers with large bikes will find it advantageous to slide the towline to the top of the head tube and secure it with a short (14 inches in length), small-gauge rope. This technique prevents the towline from sliding downward towards the front brake. Before hooking up your dog, be sure the small rope allows the towline slipknot to rotate from side to side without binding.

*Towline secured with
small-gauge rope*

Many new mountain bikes are manufactured with large diameter aluminum tubes. Smaller frame sizes may have a limited amount of space behind the head tube to accommodate the towline and permit free rotation. If the juncture behind your bike head tube offers limited space or forms a shape that is not conducive to free towline rotation, consider looping the towline around the base of your handlebar stem instead. For bikes with new-style stems, this means looping around the spacers situated below the stem; for older-style bikes, this involves wrapping around the base of the stem itself. Secure the towline in place, if necessary, with the small-gauge rope and confirm that your bike's spacers, headset cups, and stem base will not cut into the towline. These parts can have sharp edges.

Some bikejorers will find it's not possible to connect the towline to the head tube or base of the stem due to front brake, stem or frame design. In these cases, the towline must be connected to the end of the stem where the stem attaches to the handlebars. This connection point is least desirable because it affords your dog significant control over your steering. For example, if your dog bolts off-trail, the stem and wheel will immediately turn in the same direction while your center of gravity will move the opposite way. This is unnerving at first but can be controlled by quickly turning and leaning in the direction your dog is pulling. If you use this alternative, practice with a human helper so that you can experience this sensation *before* hooking up your dog.

Practicing before hooking up to a dog

Before hitting the trail with your dog, practice feathering the brakes by having a friend or family member pull you around the yard. Your surrogate canine can wear a skijor belt backwards so it's comfortable for him or her to pull. Remember that the towline is like a big rubber band, so if the snap is released under tension it will fling towards you at a high rate of speed. If you haven't yet met your neighbors, this activity may provide a suitable icebreaker. They're certain to be curious. If you're already acquainted, this may simply confirm their suspicions about you. Following are some additional exercises you can try with the assistance of your helper.

Find a small hill, preferably one with a paved surface. Have your helper pull you up one side and down the other. Avoid using your brakes in this exercise until the last moment. Note how the towline elongates up the hill and recoils on the descent to a certain point, then falls slack. A limp line is to be avoided in bikejoring! Try the exercise again, but this time feather the brakes on the downhill section to keep the towline taut and away from the front wheel.

Now that your surrogate sled dog is warmed up, have him pull you straight down a sidewalk or bike path, then abruptly off to one side or the other. Practice this maneuver until you become comfortable reacting to the lateral force. The idea is to simulate the effect of a dog bolting off-trail. Practice leaning against the lateral force on the line and steering as straight as possible without overleaning. On a loose trail, your front wheel can slip out if you lean too much. If you have a big dog or plan to run two or three at once, you'll find it's necessary to steer towards the dog(s) to stay upright. Feel free to shout ON BY to your helper and have him continue pulling forward to repeat the exercise on the other side.

Try the exercise again, but this time come to a complete stop as quickly as possible when your helper pulls to the side. You'll find it's necessary to simultaneously regulate braking pressure, lean angle and steer angle to stop quickly. Occasionally during bikejoring, a dog will bolt off the trail and around an obstacle, for example, a tree or sign. To avoid "splitting the obstacle" with your dog, you'll need to begin braking before your bike is lined up directly behind your dog. Off-balance braking like this is tricky but saves precious stopping distance as you align your bike and correct your balance for hard braking. Be sure to shout WHOA to your helper.

Have your helper pull you around a 90-degree turn. Note how the towline angle falls inside the turning radius of your bike. Imagine what happens if a tree is positioned there! Steer wide like a semi driver to avoid hitting obstacles or rubbing them with the towline on the inside of turns. With some bikes, it's also possible for the towline to catch on the handlebars or brake levers during a sharp turn. If this happens to your bike, practice undoing the tangle quickly or braking to a complete stop. It's nearly impossible to continue bikejoring when the line is caught on the handlebar or brake lever. The bike will veer in one direction and your center of balance will shift to the opposite side.

By now your helper is probably exhausted and deserves a beverage (he might not even require "baited" water in his bowl!). If he is good for another pull, have him head down the trail at a fast clip and then stop abruptly without warning. Stop directly behind, and take note of how little reaction time you have, even when you're anticipating the stop. This situation can occur when a dog catches a hot scent in the middle of the trail or feels an overwhelming need for a nature break. Both of these challenges can be remedied with training, but the latter usually requires a team size of three or more. In larger teams dogs "drop" on the run.

Now repeat the exercise, but this time practice steering around your helper as you brake to a stop. Normally it's possible to stop directly behind your dog in bikejoring if you have good brakes and traction, but we recommend making a habit of braking to the side for added security. Besides the obvious risk of injury, a dog hit from behind will lose confidence running in front.

Bikejoring with Your Dog

The next step is to hook up your dog and try an inaugural ride. Keep your first bikejor trip fairly short, and choose a cool day for the benefit of your dog. You may hit a nice cruising speed after a quarter mile or so and sense a harmony of motion that beckons for more. After all, your dog will probably relish the feeling of running on the trail at a brisk pace. Resist the temptation to push on for anything more than an introductory run at a moderate pace. Your dog will most likely be running at a speed that exceeds what you can do on foot or perhaps even on skis, and she might tire relatively quickly. It makes little sense to charge ahead for two miles, only to have the return become progressively slower, and end with your canine companion tired instead of yearning for more. A better approach is to increase your distance gradually, while paying close attention to how your dog is running on any given day.

HOOKING UP A SINGLE DOG TO BIKE

▸ Connect towline to bike head tube
▸ Check brakes and steering
▸ Lay towline out and untangle if necessary
▸ Harness dog, connect to towline and follow bike mounting sequence below

Hooking Up 2 or 3 Dogs to Bike
▸ Connect towline to bike head tube
▸ Check brakes and steering

> ▸ Secure bike to solid object such as a car bumper with snub line (a restraining line) and quick-release snap. Position snub line around seat post. Line should remain attached to bumper when released.
> ▸ Lay out towline and untangle if necessary
> ▸ Harness dogs and hook up one at a time
> ▸ Follow bike mounting sequence below
>
> *Note:* If hooking up two dogs without snub line, stand on towline after hooking up first dog while hooking up second dog (weight of skijorer, shoe tread, ground conditions, and other factors determine how well line stays in place).

Bike Mounting Sequence

After you've hooked up your dog to your bike, follow these steps to safely mount your bike.

- Never let go of your dog, line or bike, or your bike may start down the trail without you. This is especially important when using two or more dogs.

- If your dog responds well to SIT and STAY, simply give the commands and mount your bike, but be careful until you're seated with your hands on the brakes. Your dog may lunge forward before you're situated and either pull the tip of the seat into your back, or, if you're grasping the brakes, lift the rear end of your bike forward. This action will force the top tube into your groin.

- Avoid the scenarios above by first following the line from your dog back to your bike. Next, hold the bike by having one hand tightly grasping the front brake lever, so that the front wheel is locked. Put the other hand on the seat to apply downward pressure to keep the rear end of the bike down if your dog lunges.

- Now, with your hand on the front of the seat, lift one leg up and over and sit down on the seat with the other leg still anchored on the ground.

- Once your weight is on the seat, immediately grab the rear brake lever and give your dog the LINE OUT command to pull the line taut.

▸ A moment or two later, give the LET'S GO command and lift up the anchor leg.

Try a route or trail that your dog is familiar with, so that he has a good sense of where to go. To minimize distractions, you may want to make the initial run at a time when the route is not heavily used. You will have plenty to do on this trip; the less outside stimulation, the better.

Bikejoring works best when a dog already has pulling experience and consistently stays out front. For dogs that are strong pullers, you may need to brake during the entire outing. Of course you'll have the opportunity to assist by pedaling up steeper hills and on slow trail surfaces, but your primary role will be to maintain control of your team.

Bikejorers with recreational pullers will find more effort is re-

clouds in the sky today. Oh well, I'm busy concentrating on bikejoring with the dogs and have little time for meteorological speculations. Bowser and Spot quickly hit their stride, and I'm consumed with how well they are working together. So well, in fact, that it's necessary to apply steady brake pressure to control their speed.

After a very satisfying run we return to the car for watering and cooling down. While removing the dogs' harnesses, I notice numerous red spots on my dark green jacket. We're not talking a few spots, but more like 75 to 100 small crimson dots. "What in the world?" I mutter as I look in the van's side mirror, noticing that my face is also covered with the same mysterious red specks.

A close examination of the dogs' feet dismisses my rain shower theory: it was actually a light blood shower. Unbeknownst to me, my dogs wore their toenails down to the quick when they ran in place, and ground them further as we headed towards the second dirt trail. No warning was signaled by the dogs; their speed and enthusiasm were undiminished and their gait unchanged the entire run.

I was horrified by the discovery, and wasn't able to run the dogs for a couple of weeks to allow ample time for recovery. But the valuable lesson endures and is shared here to spare others a similar experience (and you can quote me on this one): "Asphalt was designed for cars, so use sparingly with dogs that pull hard, and no canine-calisthenics or running in place!" Most dogs should probably have booties on their feet if they will be running on asphalt for any distance, or if snow cover is light.

quired by the cyclist. You'll need to monitor your speed closely to avoid a slack towline. Feather your brakes to reduce slack when your dog slows or as you ride downhill sections. As you become proficient, you'll be able to maintain a more constant pace by anticipating the required braking action. Initially, however, you'll find yourself alternating between pedaling and braking in pursuit of a taut towline—not really a model of efficiency but critical for safety. Be patient as you and your dog learn to work together as a team.

Alert other trail users that you are approaching from behind so that they are not startled. When passing or meeting oncoming traffic, slow down but keep moving so that your dog isn't tempted to stop. By passing at a controlled speed, you'll be able to react quickly and successfully to avoid potential problems. Try to be a good ambassador for bikejoring by being courteous toward other trail users.

BOWSER

We're anxiously awaiting the return to cooler, darker days so we can run again in the snow. Many humans wouldn't understand, what with their thin skin and scarce patches of fur, that we run much better in cold weather! We simply can't cool ourselves as well with our tongues in warm weather. Never did comprehend why people flock to beaches, unless of course there are waterfowl in sight.

Anyway, so one day when the days are getting shorter, Thor comes up with another of his crazy but promising ideas. He hooks Spot and me up to his two-wheeled pedal-driven chariot, which he regularly rides around the neighborhood. This contraption has been great for him, since it allows him to overcome his disadvantage of two legs and even keep up with us. (Provided we stick to the trail. We caused a terrible mess once when we darted off-trail after a "bunny snack" and he attempted to follow.)

We get pretty pumped about pulling his chariot, and have trouble restraining ourselves as he's hooking us up. Man, it's great to be in harness again, but he takes so long to get moving that we have a couple of false starts. On the second one, we're all set to roar down the trail when a she-human comes up from behind him. We're concerned that they'll have to mate. Swift action is required, so we take off down the trail again, dragging the chariot behind us. This does get his attention, and his shouting encourages us that he's once again engaged in the task at hand.

We halt to allow him to catch up, though we've hit our stride and can't afford to stop entirely. So we run in place while he's mounting the chariot. Seems to take him an eternity to climb on the darn thing. We sense that if we just run a bit harder he'll climb aboard more quickly. So we open up to about 90% throttle. Not the best choice of running surfaces—my feet begin to hurt a bit—but the adrenaline is kickin' in and we can't stop. Plus, physical comfort is secondary when we're on the trail. We finally get him moving and even persuade him to turn onto the dirt trail where we can take full advantage of our "quadra-paw" traction capabilities. We must have worn him out on this one; he didn't run us again for 14 dog weeks (about two human weeks).

Cautionary Notes for Bikejoring

Ride the trail first without your dog. Are there challenging downhill sections? Any obstacles on the trail? Tight or difficult (loose trail surface or off-camber) turns? Is the trail surface safe for your dog?

Start with a single dog. If you have two or more dogs, always try bikejoring first with one dog. Choose your best leader for your first run. Bikejoring with two or more dogs on downhill sections requires expert braking and control capabilities.

Do not use a skijor belt for bikejoring. Attach the bungee towline directly to your bike as described earlier. (See "Connecting Towline to Bike.")

Connect the bungee towline properly to your bike. Follow the instructions in "Connecting Towline to Bike" to attach the line to the head tube on your bike.

Be careful as you're preparing to start down the trail. Starting out on a bike hooked up to your dog requires caution. Review "Bike Mounting Sequence" to minimize the chances of your bike lifting up or your seat hitting you in the back as you're preparing to start.

Bring the right equipment. A helmet is essential. Eyewear is always important, because your dog can kick up dirt or gravel. And for your dog, booties can be critical on hard road surfaces or rocky trails.

Maintain traction and control on downhill sections. Your dog should respond to EASY and WHOA, or you will be forced to rely entirely on your brakes. Bikejoring down hills can be precarious. Even on good trails, control may be compromised when a dog is assisting you on downward slopes. Loose surfaces or wet trails can further reduce control, making it difficult to keep your dog's speed in check.

Monitor the towline. Bikejorers cannot take their attention off the towline for even an instant. Slack line can develop quickly, tangle with the front wheel, and cause a crash. If your dog won't stay in front, bikejor with an SMA.

Minimize potential for overheating. Bikejoring is typically done in temperatures above freezing, so be cognizant of your dog's increased need for water. Remember that dogs don't sweat, they pant, so don't hesitate to let your dog take a quick break in the lake on warmer days. Make sure that you have plenty of water available for your dog before, during and after your trip. Ride in the morning or in the evening, or along a tree-shaded trail if the sun is directly overhead. If it's too warm for bikejoring, a better plan is to read a skijoring book or watch a dog movie, and do your bikejoring when it is cooler.

Cool down properly. On a warm day, the time immediately following your run is critical for your dog; this is when body temperatures can soar. Your dog must have shade, air flow and cool but not ice-cold water. Never leave your dog alone after a warm-weather workout until you're certain that she has cooled down properly.

Control your speed. Be careful not to exceed a speed appropriate for the trail conditions. Controlling your speed and knowing your limits will help avoid injury to you and your dog. Allow your dog to throttle up on safe stretches of trail only after a good warm-up.

Increase distance gradually. Don't start out attempting a 10-mile ride for your first bikejoring experience. Start with small, manageable excursions and then ratchet up gradually. This allows your dog time to safely build cardiovascular and muscular fitness. A conservative approach will leave your dog mentally refreshed and looking forward to the next run. It also provides the opportunity to gauge water requirements and monitor pad and toenail condition.

Caveats aside, bikejoring is a great option for dog and human when snow is hard to find. Bikejoring allows you to explore numerous trails in your area, offering many variations in scenery, trail surfaces and terrain. Many bikejoring trails are enjoyed by other trail users, providing added excitement and opportunities for training and socializing your dog. Take the time to read and practice the recommendations described above, and have fun with your dog!

Rollerjoring

Rollerjoring, as the name implies, combines inline skating or rollerskiing with running your dog. Sometimes referred to as skatejoring, rollerjoring is canicross with inline skates or rollerskis.

For safety reasons, we recommend trying canicross first; controlling or stopping your dog is easier when in your running shoes. Once you are comfortable with canicross, adding inline skates or rollerskis can increase your speed and excitement and more closely resemble skijoring. Note: see the section below on cautions and risks inherent to rollerjoring, and do *not* attempt this sport unless you are certain that you are able to accept responsibility for both your dog's and your own personal safety.

If you have never inline skated or rollerskied before, practice without your dog until you are comfortable and in complete control. You will need to be able to stop, control your speed and turn without hesitation. You will also need to provide resistance or

backward tension to your dog, in order to reinforce commands like EASY or WHOA. Your skates or skis must have a working brake to safely control your dog, or at a minimum, you should be able to do a snowplow step stop. As in most trail sports, the safety valve of last resort is to simply fall down. This provides tremendous incentive to maintain control when rollerjoring, since the trail surface (usually pavement or gravel) is significantly less cushioning and more abrasive on impact than snow.

You can use your regular inline skates or rollerskis if you plan to rollerjor on pavement, though it is preferable to use off-road styles. With them, you can take your dog rollerjoring on gravel or dirt trails as well. Rollerjoring on pavement requires that you pay special attention to the pads and nails on your dog's feet. Depending on his pulling characteristics, your dog may need booties when running on pavement, and you may need to limit the distance covered on hard surfaces. Using off-road trails helps preserve pads and toenails. Keep in mind, though, that your dog may still need booties. See Chapter 6, "Equipment," for information about booties.

Another point in favor of off-road skates and rollerskis is that they provide a softer ride; the larger diameter wheels roll more easily over debris on any kind of trail. The best trails are packed dirt or smooth gravel, relatively flat, and infrequently used. They're safer for the rollerjorer and easier on your dog's feet. For both you and your dog, these trails provide a more pleasant and scenic experience. Off-road gear gives you the choice.

For further preparation and planning, see "Cautionary Notes Specific to Rollerskiing," at the end of this chapter, before attempting to rollerski with your dog.

Line length should be comparable to that used for skijoring with a single dog. The shorter length used in canicross is generally not sufficient for the skating technique and increased stopping distances required in rollerjoring.

Equipment vendors offer a tow rope handle so you can rollerjor without attaching the towline to your skijor belt. This allows you to drop the handle in an emergency situation, essentially as a last resort. Resembling a water-ski tow handle, it helps reduce risks for beginners and increases safety if city streets and traffic are unavoidable. This is not intended as a complete solution, since releasing the handle at an intersection might save you but send your dog into traffic. Rollerjoring with the towline attached to the belt should be reserved for very experienced rollerjorers who know their dogs and, just as importantly, the route they will travel.

If you plan to connect your dog to your skijor belt, choose a trail without *any* motor vehicle traffic—preferably one with grass on either side for emergency stops. It's also important to rollerjor when other trail traffic is light, including wildlife! Since it's impossible to avoid rabbits and squirrels, make sure your dog responds well to verbal commands so you can maintain control when Brer Rabbit darts across the trail. Finally, wear a helmet and other protective gear to reduce the potential for injury should a spill occur.

Let your dog run on the grass beside the trail if possible. Many dogs will actually choose grass over pavement. If you have an energetic dog that likes to pull hard and run fast, it's very important to make sure the trail is safe. This is especially important in the first mile, when you'll be traveling the fastest, so a trail that starts on a downhill stretch with sharp turns would be a poor choice. A trail that begins with a steady uphill section is preferred because it helps minimize your initial speed.

Rollerjoring is the most dangerous of any skijoring-related dog-powered sport. The following list of risks and cautions should be taken seriously, and rollerjoring should not be attempted if there is any question about your ability or resolve to properly address any of these issues.

Risk Factors and Cautionary Notes for Rollerjoring

Difficulty in stopping quickly. Inline skates and rollerskis are not designed to stop both you and a dog that is pulling out front. You must be able to stop as quickly as possible, using your skates' or skis' braking mechanism. Inline skaters have the option of dragging a foot to slow down, although this alternative is less effective than using a brake and it requires a high degree of skill.

Hard and abrasive landing surface. Rollerjorers and bike racers sometimes refer to "road rash" as the byproduct of an unscheduled brush with the pavement. *Wear a helmet* and appropriate padding on knees, elbows and hands, but be aware that they reduce but do not eliminate the risk of injury.

Traffic. Don't rollerjor in traffic! Avoid city streets and intersections whenever possible. Could you stop if your dog sees a squirrel on the other side of a busy street? To avoid this situation, choose non-motorized trails with very limited pedestrian traffic. If your dog attempts to pull you into traffic, fall down.

Towline versus belt. Unless you are an accomplished inline skater or rollerskier with verbal control over your dog, do not use a skijor belt to rollerjor. Instead, hold the towline until you are completely comfortable rollerjoring with your dog. Practice operating the belt quick-release several times before hooking up your dog.

Wet pavement. Your ability to stop, control your speed or turn is virtually eliminated when pavement is wet. Wait until surfaces are dry.

Less reaction time. Compared to canicross, you will have far less time to react or make decisions. And Murphy's tenets apply very well to rollerjoring. For example, if you expect your dog to go around a pole in the middle of the trail (the kind that keeps cars off bike trails) and you expect your dog to GEE around the pole, he will HAW. By this time, you can't change your direction, so the center of the rope hits the pole and you both do an emergency stop. Therefore, anticipate any decisions (and corresponding commands) you will have to make as far ahead as possible.

Lack of understanding of necessary commands. Work with your dog on commands when doing canicross or skijoring to make sure that you both understand them, before trying rollerjoring.

Use of multiple dogs. Rollerjoring with more than one dog is *not* recommended. Use a single dog.

Minimize potential for overheating. Rollerjoring is typically done above freezing, so be cognizant of your dog's increased need for water. Remember that dogs don't sweat, they pant, so don't hesitate to let your dog take a quick break in the lake on warm days. Make sure that you have plenty of drinking water available for your dog before, during and after your trip. Rollerjor in the morning or at night, or along a tree-shaded route if the sun is directly overhead. If it's too warm for rollerjoring, a better plan is to read a skijoring book or watch a dog movie, and do your rollerjoring when it is cooler.

Cool down properly. On a warm day, the time immediately following your run is critical for your dog; this is when body temperatures can soar. Your dog must have shade, air flow and cool but not ice-cold water. Never leave your dog unattended after a warm-weather work-out until you're certain that she has cooled down properly.

Unfamiliar routes. Don't rollerjor on trails that you are not familiar with, since you will be unable to properly anticipate dangerous intersections, steep hills, sharp turns or other potential hazards. Do your exploring first on a solo trek.

Problems resulting from your dog running on pavement. The pad on your dog's foot provides great cushioning, but like humans, the dog's gene pool ancestors did not spend a minute running on concrete or asphalt. Excessive miles can contribute to impact problems similar to those humans encounter, as well as worn pads and toenails. Reread the section on booties in Chapter 6.

Bailout strategy. You should have a rehearsed action plan in case you need to make an emergency stop. If you need to implement your plan, aim for the grass. Practice this prior to hooking up your dog, since the transition to grass will likely stop your skates in their tracks.

To avoid falling forward when this happens, shift your weight backward. It also helps to have your skates shoulder-width apart and staggered (one skate forward of the other). If you're traveling at slow speed, it's possible to run onto the grass with your skates, but at higher speeds coasting "off-road" may be the best option.

If a crash is inevitable, use your arm to break your fall, but avoid stiff-arming the ground or you'll simply transfer the shock up your arm to your shoulder and collarbone. Instead, use your arm as a shock absorber by transitioning your impact into a roll.

Cautionary Notes Specific to Rollerskiing

- Because rollerskis are less maneuverable and stable than inline skates (inline skates have stiffer boots and fixed heels), you should be an experienced and proficient roller-skier before attempting this rollerjoring alternative.

- Rollerskiing adds ski poles and consequently requires the rollerskier to use the skijor belt instead of a tow handle. Note cautions discussed earlier regarding the use of the skijor belt for rollerjoring.

Off-road rollerski with pneumatic tires shown with boot

- Off-road rollerskis are best for rollerjoring with rollerskis. Some models are equipped with pneumatic (air-filled) tires, which absorb road shock and roll easily over small stones or sticks on the trail.

- Packed dirt or smooth gravel trails are preferred over pavement for rollerjoring with rollerskis, due to the inherent slower speeds and reduced potential injury from impact.

- Trails should be flat or slightly rolling, with gentle turns.

- Have a friend pull you first, as described under bikejoring ("Practicing before hooking up to a dog") so you can become acquainted with stability and control issues.

- A variable rate suspension towline is critical since the same ski techniques (V2, V2 Alternate, etc.) are used with rollerskiing as with skijoring. The variable suspension reduces the shock that can upset a rollerjorer's balance.

- As in skijoring, start without poles to get a feel for rollerjoring with rollerskis. Add poles when you're ready for the additional challenge and speed.

Rollerjoring offers the closest warm-weather approximation to skijoring in terms of movement behind the dog and type of exercise for dog and human. However, rollerjoring also carries the greatest amount of risk among skijoring-related sports due to reduced control and inability to stop quickly. For this reason, it is of paramount importance that rollerjorers have verbal control over their dog. When practiced responsibly on safe trails, rollerjoring offers an exciting outing for canine and human.

CHAPTER TEN

The *Ski Spot Run* Top 10 List

This book is an introduction to the exciting sport of skijoring and related dog-powered sports. The preceding pages have attempted to capture the beauty of the sport, the basics of technique and commands, and recommended equipment. We've included detailed instructions, action photos, and humorous illustrations to portray the "how to" aspects along with a wide breadth of experiences. Still, one book can only provide a glimpse of this unique sport. We accept this limitation, and have harnessed it to drive us toward compiling relevant and concise information. If we've validated veteran skijorers' experiences, or have persuaded beginners to give it a shot, then it was worth our time and effort.

When writing this book, we strived to adhere to what we refer to as the *Five E's:*

Entice: Our goal is to draw you into the sport, so that you will want to try skijoring if you're a newcomer, or improve if you've skijored previously. We'll consider the project a success when you put down the book, summon your dog, and head out to the trail.

Educate: We all benefit, humans and dogs alike, from an increased understanding of the sport. We've attempted to provide detail on the sport from multiple vantage points, and from both the human and probable canine perspective.

Entertain: The various vignettes and stories are just a small sample of the diverse experiences we've heard about or experienced first-hand. Many are humorous, but all are intended to provide insight and prevent possible reenactment. And though we're serious about the sport of skijoring, it sometimes helps to not take ourselves too seriously.

Encourage: Above all, we want you to give it a try. Skijoring is a sport for the mainstream, and is not limited to racers or Northern sled dogs. With a little preparation, you can do it, and your status (in your dog's eyes) will soar.

Enlist: Any successful sport requires ambassadors and stewardship. Your help is requested in promoting the best interests of skijoring, bikejoring, and other dog-powered sports, whether actively or simply by being a responsible participant.

In closing, since one of the skijoring clubs that we know of has a Top 10 List for skijoring, we decided to create our own.

The *Ski Spot Run* Top 10 List

The top 10 reasons for getting involved in sports that allow you to run, bike, in-line skate, or ski behind your dog:

  10. You enjoy the challenge of trying to calm your dog down after inadvertently showing him the harness, 10 minutes before you're ready to take him out on the trail.

   9. You need a support group for people whose dogs refuse to heel and insist on pulling out front when on walks or runs. Camaraderie with other pet owners helps ease the pain and suffering resulting from owning a dog overly intent on being the leader.

Top 10 List reason #9

"Blaze had his owner take up skijoring so he could unlearn that heeling habit. Now he gets to run up front!"

8. Your children are now out of their diapers and have left home. You miss A) training them, B) cleaning up after them, C) giving them commands which they ignore, and D) running after and trying to keep up with them. You realize that skijoring helps fill this void.

7. Your artistic side is deeply interested in doing macramé with towlines, and in creating new and innovative designer weaves with polyethylene ropes. As one owner was overheard to remark, "it takes two to tangle, but three to really tie the knot."

6. You have a secret desire to scoop up, bag, and haul manure around on ski trails, sometimes carrying it in your pocket for several hours.

5. Your "significant other" told you to hit the trail. And your dog agreed.

4. You're slightly self-conscious about running solo through your neighborhood clad in black tights. Running behind a dog immediately bestows credibility and purpose.

Top 10 List reason #3

3. You don't have enough belts in your collection. You're especially interested in one with lots of those nifty quick-release snaps and straps that wrap around your thighs and groin.

"It's the best fitting belt in my collection."

2. You have a strong need to affiliate with clandestine or obscure organizations, perhaps allowing you to fantasize about being involved with a CIA or Secret Service operation. You're especially interested in activities few people have heard of, with names that are difficult to pronounce.

1. You're tired of using the words right and left and are interested in learning new ways to express yourself that no one else in the office will comprehend. You sort of feel like John Wayne every time you scream out HAW or WHOA.

The light snow continues to fall on the trail as you ski behind your canine companion. The alpenglow from the setting sun lingers a bit longer, as you admire the fluid motion of your dog in front. You savor this place, and are fully absorbed by the wonder and beauty of the present. You feel a serenity matched by precious few earthly pursuits; a harmony virtually unrivaled.

We've evolved together in so many ways, you reflect while working with your teammate. From the time our ancestors first noticed glowing eyes near the campfire, until now. Today the partnership is still about survival, though from the human perspective it is less physical and more psychological in nature. As a team we share friendship, loyalty and simplicity in a fast-paced and complex world. Together we are more complete, and we are stronger.

You realize you don't want it to end, as you glide toward the trailhead. The towline is still tight, your dog's stride energetic, and your skis have never felt better. And now you're approaching the junction: a right turn leads to the parking lot; a left follows a short loop out and back again. Your dog knows the loop well, having warmed up and cooled down many times on the route.

You know you probably shouldn't, but tonight you'll let your dog decide. She knows that GEE leads to the car and the usual cache of treats, while HAW extends the adventure just a bit longer. You notice a fine layer of light snow collecting on her warm winter coat, and are impressed by just how exquisitely dressed she is for the occasion. You resolve to remain silent as you reach the junction, and wonder if she will pause or make a quick decision. You will be completely happy with either path chosen by your partner.

At the intersection, there is no hesitation on her part. We truly are kindred spirits. It looks like we're going around one more time.

Outtakes, *SKI SPOT RUN* Top 10 List

- The other day, your dog asked you to define "couch potato." Apparently the neighborhood dogs were at it again, gossiping about their owners. Time to nip this rumor in the bud.

- You enjoy that condescending look from your dog after falling on the trail and apparently keeping him from continuing a great run.

- Your dog has finally convinced you that she should really be the leader, pulling up front. She has agreed to let you try out for the second position, behind her, provided you're not a slacker.

- You're interested in obtaining more sporting gear and equipment to add to the clutter already present in the garage and downstairs storage area.

- You heard they would be filming a remake of Balto next season in a nearby town, and were thinking about trying out as an extra. You figure that even though you're a long shot, your dog has a fighting chance.

- You're determined to show your dog that you can pull your own weight and that you're not just a caboose but an engine as well.

- You're not quite ready to bungee jump off an abandoned bridge into a canyon. However, skijoring sounds like an appealing alternative once you learn that the bungee towline is not used for suspending your body in midair.

- You've always been a student of Murphy's Law, and in the interest of science are graciously offering to do further research on the Law's relationship to skijoring.

- Skijorers and mushers throw the best tailgate parties.

Suggested Reading

The Art of Raising a Puppy, The Monks of New Skete, Little Brown & Company, 1991

Born to Pull, Bob Cary, Gail de Marcken, Scholastic, 2003

The Complete Dog Book, American Kennel Club Staff, Howell Book House, 1998

The Complete Guide to Cross-Country Ski Preparation, Nat Brown, The Mountaineers/Cordee, 1999

Cross-Country Skiing: A Complete Guide, Brian Cazeneuve, W.W. Norton & Company, 1995

The Essential Cross-Country Skier, Rick Lovett, Paul Petersen, John Morton, International Marine/Ragged Mountain Press, 1999

Fitness Cross Country Skiing, Steven E. Gaskill, Human Kinetics, 1998

How to be Your Dog's Best Friend, The Monks of New Skete, Little Brown & Company, 2002

Husky Song, Patsy Shannon, Ryan Press, 2002

Leader of the Pack: How to Take Control of your Relationship with your Dog, Nancy Baer and Steve Duno, Quill/HarperCollins, 1996

Skijoring & Off-Season Activities, The Best of Mushing Magazine, 2001

Skijor With Your Dog, Mari Høe-Raitto and Carol Kaynor, OK Publishing, 1991

Ski Skating with Champions: How to ski with least energy, Einar Svensson, published by author, 1994

The Speed Mushing Manual: How to Train Racing Sled Dogs, Jim Welch, Sirius Publishing, 1989

The Truth About Dogs, Stephen Budiansky, Penguin Books, 2000

Waxing for Skiers, Malcolm Corcoran, Stackpole Books, 1999

Winterdance: The Fine Madness of Running the Iditarod, Gary Paulsen, Harvest Books, 1995

Index

About the Authors and Artist

Matt Haakenstad enjoys skijoring with his black lab, Sadie. In the warmer seasons they modify their routine to include canicross and bikejoring. Matt has pursued outdoor winter sports such as downhill and cross-country skiing since he was four years old. He also enjoys canoeing in Minnesota's Boundary Waters Canoe Area Wilderness, and remains active in Scouting. He is a professional engineer with U.S. Energy Services, Inc., and resides in Minnetonka, Minnesota with his wife, Lisa, and children, Mark and Annie.

John Thompson has raced competitively as a skijorer for seven seasons. In 2001 he placed 5th in the 23k event at the International Federation of Sled Dog Sports Skijoring World Championships in Fairbanks, Alaska. John also enjoys bikejoring, rollerjoring, and canicross with his Alaskan huskies, Timber and Kiska. He owns and manages Skijor Now, a skijoring equipment supply and manufacturing business. John resides in Shoreview, Minnesota with his wife, Julie, and children, Stephanie and Eric.

Jack Lunde started drawing as soon as he was old enough to crawl over and grab a pencil. His mother quickly determined that her only hope of saving their furniture and walls from his creative sketches was to provide him continual access to drawing paper. He has observed and captured human and canine behavior in his illustrations for many years. He works as a graphic artist at Swanson Health Products. Jack, his wife Nancy, and family reside in Fargo, North Dakota.

Jack, Matt, and John at work on Ski Spot Run.
PHOTO BY SPOT